D0031153

GHOSTS OF
KING SOLOMON'S
MINES

GHOSTS OF KING SOLOMON'S MINES

MOZAMBIQUE AND ZIMBABWE:
A QUEST

GRAHAM LORD

SINCLAIR-STEVENSON

First published in Great Britain by
Sinclair-Stevenson Limited
7/8 Kendrick Mews
London SW7 3HG, England

British Library Cataloguing in Publication Data
A CIP catalogue record for this book is available from the British Library.
ISBN: 1 85619 072 2

Typeset by Rowland Phototypesetting Limited
Bury St Edmunds, Suffolk
Printed and bound in Great Britain by
Butler and Tanner Limited, Frome, Somerset

For Juliet
and in memory of my mother and father,
Ida McDowall (1910–1966) and Harold Lord (1900–1969)

ACKNOWLEDGEMENTS

MY aunt Dorothy Leckie's memories, enthusiasm and encouragement have been invaluable, as have those of May Davidson, and I am particularly grateful to Denis Norman, Ian Smith, Sir Garfield and Lady Todd and Sir Roy and Lady Welensky for agreeing to interviews.

Although many of my other informants in Mozambique and Zimbabwe prefer sadly to remain anonymous, I can at least thank the following publicly for all their practical help and guidance, for which I am immensely grateful:

Ibraimo Adamo, John Edlin, Ian Ehlinger, Vic Ferreira, Marguerita Furtado, Michael Hammond, Jack Harrison, Liz Henderson, Jan and Colette Hendrikse, John Hillis, Claude Mellor, Mary Mitchel, Miss T. J. Moyo, Glandeur Sibotshiwe, Laurie Sparham, Judith Todd, Neil Todd, Bibi Umarjee, Justin Walford, Derek Wilson, George and Dorothy Wilson.

I would also like to thank Robin Morgan (then editing the *Sunday Express*) and Sue Peart, Editor of the *Sunday Express* magazine, for encouraging me to return to Africa in 1990 and for publishing a short version of Chapter 1 in the magazine. A brief version of Chapter 9 was also published by Dominic Lawson in *The Spectator*.

CONTENTS

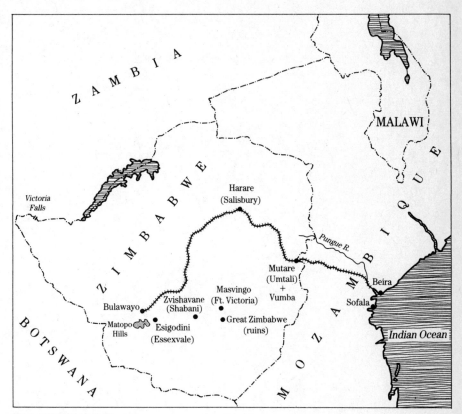

Ghosts of King Solomon's Mines

RETURN TO AFRICA

NONE OF US ever completely escapes the influences of childhood, and for a writer especially those early years are a compost heap of neuroses that fertilise the work no matter how different each book may seem to be.

My own childhood seemed enchanted because it was spent in Central Africa in the fabulous lands long connected with *King Solomon's Mines* – Zimbabwe and Mozambique – and I was there during the heyday of the British and Portuguese empires, in the 1940s and 1950s, when Zimbabwe was still the British colony of Southern Rhodesia and Mozambique was still known as PEA: Portuguese East Africa. I was born and schooled at Umtali, a few miles from the Rezende gold mine that legend says was the original mine of King Solomon, near the River Sabi that is said to have given its name to the Queen of Sheba. To the west is the eerie, brooding ruin of Great Zimbabwe, once perhaps a staging post for medieval Arab slave traders and gold and ivory merchants on their way to the dhows awaiting them at Sofala on the coast of the Indian Ocean. And to the east my home in Mozambique was just up the coast from Sofala, which some believe was the 'Ophir' that John Masefield mentioned in his poem *Cargoes*:

> Quinquireme of Nineveh from distant Ophir
> Rowing home to haven in sunny Palestine,
> With a cargo of ivory,
> And apes and peacocks,
> Sandalwood, cedarwood, and sweet white wine.

When I left both Mozambique and Zimbabwe in 1960 at the age of seventeen to go up to Cambridge I fully intended to return after three years at university. Where else should I go? Central Africa was all I knew. My pioneering Scottish grandfather, Alexanda McDowall from Glenluce – a descendant of the warlike 'wild Irish' M'Douls of Scotia and the M'Dowalls that founded Balliol College (Oxford) and challenged Robert the Bruce for the Scottish throne, the 'wild Scots' sheep-stealing McDowalls of Galloway – had run the first Meikle's department store in Umtali after trekking hundreds of miles north through the bush from South Africa in the 1890s. He had served as a councillor on Umtali's first town council while his brother Andrew McDowall was fathering my Hollywood actor cousin Roddy McDowall's father Tom, who seemed to believe that we were the rightful kings of Britain. My mother had been born in Umtali and I had spent seven years at a very English prep school nearby, in the beautiful Vumba mountains that slouch at dusk like quiet blue giants on the primitive Mozambique border. I had gone on to public school a few miles outside Lobengula's old Matabele kraal city of Bulawayo. And home was still the surprisingly British town of Beira in Portuguese East Africa, on the idyllic shore of the Indian Ocean, where my Essex-born father had been a shipping agent with the Beira Boating Company and the Manica Trading Company since 1928. Where else but to Africa should I return after three years at Cambridge? Before I left I signed up to serve my two years' compulsory national service in the Rhodesian army on my return.

But England and Cambridge quickly won my heart, and so did an English girl called Jane. I worked as a gardener at a royal mansion in Windsor Great Park, Cumberland Lodge, and as a teacher at a prep school in Cirencester, as a night porter at a hotel in Colchester, as a reporter on the *Cambridge Evening News*. I married and had two very English daughters. I landed the job of my dreams in Fleet Street as Literary Editor of the *Sunday Express*. I published six very English novels and although in four of them I returned compulsively to Africa, like a man licking the empty root of a pulled tooth, it seemed by then no longer a place to take a young family. In 1965 Ian Smith declared Southern Rhodesia independent of Britain and swore that Rhodesia would never see black majority rule in a thousand years. My conscripted Rhodesian friends were being parachuted into the bush to kill black men who only wanted the vote and some dignity. My contemporaries were dying on the Mozambique border, and in 1978 my little prep school in the Vumba was the scene of a dreadful massacre of white missionaries and their children.

In Mozambique the black Frelimo guerrillas won their war of independence and threw the Portuguese out to set up a ramshackle Marxist state dominated by grim Russian and East German 'advisers' and a distrust of the West – especially of Western journalists. One of my father's successors as general manager of the Manica Trading Company in Beira was accused of sabotage, of blowing up oil tanks, of being a South African agent, and was sentenced to twenty years in the unimaginable hell of Mozambican prisons. How could I go back? My Africa no longer existed.

Yet for thirty years I dreamed of it, and my novels kept dragging me back. For thirty years I tramped the busy streets of London and the trim silent Surrey suburbs and the high wide windswept racing downs of Berkshire and fantasised about returning one day to the sweaty equator to dig into the festering compost heap of memory. In sleep I wandered again along the palmy sandy shores of the Indian Ocean, through the blazing tropical gardens and the cool verandahs of my childhood. I dreamed of the beauties of the veld and mountain streams and wallowed in recollections of dusty corridors and chalky classrooms where once I had wondered what I might become. Each year for thirty years I postponed going back. I felt that my roots had been mutilated.

But in 1990, at last, I returned, exactly a hundred years after the first Rhodesian pioneers had raised the Union Jack at Fort Salisbury (now Harare) in 1890. Zimbabwe was once again at peace after the nightmare of its long civil war – a bloody war not only of blacks against whites but later, even after independence, of blacks against blacks, when the flat brown veld around Bulawayo saw the Matabele descendants of Lobengula's proud Zulu impis in battle once again. This time it was not with the glinting spears and chilling throaty chants of their ancestors but with silent knives and petrol bombs and Kalashnikovs as they fought to preserve something of their faded power and influence against the ascendancy of President Mugabe's exultant Shona tribe whom their Matabele ancestors had for so long despised.

Mozambique too was at last accessible again. In desperation after years of civil war and dreadful poverty it had finally turned its back on the failure of its fifteen-year Marxist experiment and was encouraging Western investment and tourism, even Western journalists. After thirty years my visa to return to Mozambique took just one week to come through.

My return to Africa was unforgettable for me. So much had changed but so much was the same. My visit to Zimbabwe coincided with the moment when the sun was finally setting on the British Empire in Africa: the Lancaster House agreement with Britain, the last tattered fragment of British legal authority in Africa, which had for ten years safeguarded the rights of Ian Smith's rebel white Rhodesian minority, was about to expire the next month. Mugabe had already abolished the upper house, the Senate, and done away with the parliamentary seats reserved for whites, and now he was fighting a general election which (in theory at least) would allow him at last to uproot the British-made constitution, set up a one-party Marxist state, seize white-owned land and give it to blacks, and perhaps declare himself president for life.

While I was in Harare Mugabe was basking in the reflected glory of Nelson Mandela, who was making his first visit to Zimbabwe after his release from prison. There were speeches, a party political rally, motorcades. Yet Mugabe was facing severe opposition not only from the still powerful fat-cat whites who continue to live there like millionaires but also from

Africans contemptuous of his plans to establish a one-party state at the very moment that Eastern Europe was throwing off its one-party chains. Some Africans were muttering openly about a leader so blind to the realities of the modern world that he made a speech praising 'my good friend Nicolai Ceausescu', the evil tyrant of Romania, just a day before Ceausescu was toppled.

In a curious way, despite Mugabe's apparently immense power and his flashy presidential motorcades, he seems at sixty-six to be almost irrelevant to the future of Zimbabwe, a brave but fading Cheshire Cat face from the past. His war of independence and his very real achievement in reconciling the tribes and races have thrown up a young, intelligent black middle class that is not at all impressed by his Marxist dreams and wants to be part of the real world. They no longer see themselves as fighting old battles against Ian Smith and the spectre of white supremacy. Despite all Mugabe's Marxist rhetoric, Zimbabwe is still a lush and blessed land that he himself once described to Smith as 'the jewel of Africa'.

I confess that when I revisited my prep school in Zimbabwe and my childhood home in Mozambique I wept – but on each occasion for different reasons. This book tries to explain why.

After weeks in the sun refertilising my roots I came back to London with hundreds of pages of diary notes and hours of taped interviews. Ian Smith had spoken to me openly and with bitterness at his chintzy suburban home in Harare. Smith's sworn enemy, Mugabe's missionary friend Sir Garfield Todd (the first white liberal Southern Rhodesian Prime Minister, now eighty-one) had given me lunch at his remote Hokonui ranch and talked of the help he had given the black guerrillas during the civil war that could easily have had him hanged by Smith for treason. Senators, politicians, journalists, businessmen and farmers explained what has happened in the country of my birth – as did the former Prime Minister Sir Roy Welensky after I returned to Britain. And in twitchy Mozambique I learned to ask questions quietly, to hide my camera in a plastic British Airways carrier bag, and not to quote my sources by name.

Zimbabwe and Mozambique share a strong British heritage but while Zimbabwe is still surprisingly civilised and efficient, Mozambique has sunk into an abyss of Fourth World poverty and desperation. Together they represent the two extremes of modern independent Africa – the new light and dark, the new black and white. Both face challenges and opportunities which could perhaps one day see their roles reversed. In Zimbabwe the jungle still threatens to encroach; in Mozambique there is a flicker of hope lightening the horizon. For me they are not only dusty souvenirs of my past but also signposts marking the new millennium and the first century when Africans and Europeans may at last be able to face each other as equals.

In a hotel room in the town where I was born, Umtali (now Mutare), I heard one midnight from a nearby radio the muffled, haunting strains of Africa's continental prayer and national anthem, *Nkosi Sikelel'i Afrika* – which is sung in Shona as *Ishe Komberera Africa* – a hymn that nowadays they sing with pride, both blacks and whites, even at my posh public school in the bush near Bulawayo:

Ishe komberera Africa! God Bless Africa.
Ngaisimudzirwe zita rayo. Let its name be uplifted.
Inzwai miteuro yedu, Hear our prayers,
Isu Mhuri yayo. We, the children of Africa.

We of the white African tribe in exile can only murmur 'Amen'.

PART ONE

ZIMBABWE

CHAPTER 1

'THE JEWEL OF AFRICA'

AT 8.30 p.m. in the stillness of a black African night, on Friday 23 June 1978, a nightmare came brutally true on the pretty cricket field of my tiny, remote but very English prep school in the Vumba mountains of eastern Rhodesia. From out of the sinister bush of the Mozambique border five miles away there emerged a silent gang – probably some of Robert Mugabe's black freedom fighters, who were soon to win their war against Ian Smith and his 250,000 white Rhodesians.

The terrorists slipped through the darkness into the cosy, manicured Eagle School grounds from the direction of the Top Gate, where in 1953 we had lined up in our grey flannel shorts and navy blue blazers (with the gold Eagle badge and Latin motto *Arduus ad Solem*) to wave Union Jacks at the Queen Mother. The guerrillas skirted above the little valley with its gurgling mountain-stream swimming pool beside the grassy open-air stage, where every year we put on a Shakespeare play (to the lyrical strains of *Greensleeves* wafting across the African jungle) and where in 1956 my Malvolio took the Vumba by storm.

They slunk in beside the gravel drive where devoted masters like Claude de Clegg Mellor from the Dragon School, Oxford, had first come thirty years before to set up a replica in the sun. They padded across the trim English lawns where we had played Open Gates and let off our fireworks on Guy Fawkes night. They crept past the chalky classrooms where we struggled with French and Algebra and stood up to chorus 'Good morning, sir' whenever a master or visitor entered.

They passed the tuckshop where we bought for a ha'penny each black gobstoppers unfortunately known as nigger-balls. They invaded the dormitories where we had slouched about on lazy Sunday afternoons reading comics, *The Beano*, *The Dandy*, *Eagle*. They yelled Marxist harangues at the terrified pupils and stormed through the hall where the walls were hung with polished honours boards listing long-gone School Captains, scholarships, winners of the Gold Medal – where so often we had warbled the school song to the tune of *Onward Christian Soldiers*.

Then they seized nine white teachers, all from England -- three men and six women – and their four tiny children, and marched them out into the night through the leafy glade of acacia trees where we had played loud games of rounders and roasted noisy sausages over open fires on the Queen's Birthday.

On the edge of the cricket field, beside the pavilion, a few yards from the scoreboard with its white-on-black metal numbers clanking in the breeze, the black terrorists raped the white women and girls and then slaughtered all thirteen, even the three-week-old baby Pamela Lynn, who was bayoneted. One man was bludgeoned to death with logs. One woman died with an axe buried in the back of her head. Others were stabbed and mutilated. One child was found the next day in her blood-soaked nightdress with small yellow flowers on it, her stiff fingers clutching for her dead mother's hand an inch away.

What made the carnage especially dreadful was that all the teachers at Eagle – by then called the Elim Mission School – were peaceful missionaries, unarmed, and the pupils were no longer 110 rich, privileged, white boys but 250 black boys and girls who might otherwise never have had any education. It is said that during the massacre the missionaries tried to sing hymns.

The horror at Eagle that night was not simply one random episode of unthinkable evil, now best forgotten. At the time it symbolised the pointless carnage of that terrible civil war, and in Britain the story was splashed over the front pages and caused a major row in the Commons over Labour Foreign Secretary David Owen's policy on terrorism in Rhodesia.

In fact, by some odd quirk of coincidence, the history of Eagle School, even now, mirrors the history of white Rhodesia and its reincarnation as black Zimbabwe.

In the British colonial era the school was so incredibly English that we all spoke with BBC accents. In the war of black liberation it was the scene of one of the war's most appalling atrocities, which Robert Mugabe later blamed on Ian Smith's security forces, claiming it was a dirty disinformation exercise, as Mugabe still blames Smith for so much even now – a charge which Smith of course denied vociferously when I asked him about it at his home in Harare.

For years afterwards the school was closed and empty, as so much of white Rhodesia/Zimbabwe seemed closed and empty then, and no local African would go near the place: they said it was haunted; they said that at night you could hear the singing of hymns coming from the cricket field.

After Comrade Mugabe came to power in 1980 – and two-thirds of the whites began to leave the country, alarmed by his Marxist rhetoric – my cosy little old English prep school in the Vumba became a secret restricted area run by North Korean soldiers, with eyes like pebbles, who used it to train Mugabe's new army. As white fears failed to materialise, and the surprisingly statesmanlike Comrade Mugabe resisted the temptation to hang Ian Smith from the nearest lamp-post and instead preached forgiveness, it became a school again, run by the Ministry of Youth, Sport and Culture.

Today, amazingly, Eagle School is once again called Eagle. Its pupils are no longer white boys aged six to thirteen, learning Shakespeare and Latin, but twenty-year-old black girls training to be secretaries. There's no longer a portrait of the Queen in the headmaster's study but one of President Comrade Mugabe – and a faded poster of Lenin ordering workers of the world to unite. Otherwise remarkably little has changed.

The grounds and buildings are exactly the same. Even the blue iron beds in the dormitories are the ones we slept on forty years ago, and the same school hand-bell is rung. The head of Eagle today – fat, jolly Miss Moyo – gives me tea and delicate tomato sandwiches under the poster of Lenin and giggles about needing to diet. When I walk into the classrooms the girls stand up and chorus 'Good morning, sir.' The head girl, Glandeur Sibotshiwe, is a striking, sassy twenty-two-year-old Zulu, but she is just as proud of the school as we were. 'We still call Eagle "Little England",' she says. The school tuckshop is now in the old cricket pavilion, just a yard from the scene of the massacre: it's closed, but I bet it still sells nigger-balls, though doubtless they're called something else nowadays. On the field nearby the girls play rounders, as we did, and the cricket scoreboard still reads unconvincingly: '1st Innings 466, Last Man 268.'

The extraordinary time-warp survival of 'Little England' at Eagle School, despite all that has happened, is not an aberration. It is typical of modern Zimbabwe. Wherever I went, throughout the country, I felt that apart from all the black faces I was back in 1950s suburban England. Up in the Vumba mountains, where Mozambican guerrillas still cross the border now and then to rape and kill, there are dinky bungalows called Chatsworth and Dunromin. The fabulous Leopard Rock Hotel, with its fairytale towers, once the epitome of 1950s elegance, will open again next year, though at the moment the Queen Mum's 1953 room is chipped and peeling and her bath is stained with rust. Many Africans speak an ultra-correct, old-fashioned English that hasn't been heard in Britain for thirty years. My birthplace, Mutare, has few white faces today, but the streets are much tidier than the streets of London, the municipal gardens are spruce and colourful, the war memorial is lovingly tended and there's a red English pillarbox outside the Mutare Club where they made part of the film *Cry Freedom* and where my grandfather was Chairman in 1920 and red-faced whites in khaki shorts still sip sundowners at dusk. At 6 p.m. in the cocktail bar of the Manica Hotel, despite the heat, the African drinkers are immaculately dressed and the black barman asks me politely to leave for not wearing a tie.

It's Little England, without a doubt. The Zimbabwe AA's offices are all called Fanum House, as they are in Britain. There's racing at Newmarket and Ascot (Bulawayo), and in Harare the England A cricket team is batting as drearily as ever in the First 'Test'. Black schoolgirls wear jaunty straw boaters and the Andy Capp cartoon strip appears in the Bulawayo *Chronicle*. Zimbabwe today is a sort of sunny, black-faced 1950s Woking.

Ian Smith says that when Robert Mugabe succeeded him as Prime Minister of this beautiful land Mugabe described it as 'the Jewel of Africa', and when President Nyerere of Tanzania first visited Zimbabwe in 1981 he told Mugabe in awe: 'You have inherited a jewel ... don't tarnish it.' Certainly it's impossible to believe that this could ever be the grim one-party Marxist state of which President Comrade Mugabe dreams, despite the identical solemn portraits of Mugabe that hang on the walls of every school, office, hotel, bar, café, supermarket and department store. The imperialist statues have been pulled down and the colonial names of many streets have been altered to honour the heroes of the black revolution. While I was in Harare they finally got around after ten years of independence to changing Rhodes Avenue, the wide boulevard that for nearly a hundred years commemorated the arch-imperialist of them all, Cecil Rhodes: it's now called Herbert Chitepo Avenue. But Harare's black taxi-drivers are not impressed. They'll be calling it Rhodes Avenue for many years, they say. Why confuse people? they ask. Who was Herbert Chitepo, anyway?

In the swank Harare Club – still dominated by prosperous white businessmen who have somehow managed to hang on to their immense wealth and their big houses, lush gardens, swimming pools, Mercedes, silver, cut glass and swarms of black servants in crisp white uniforms, white gloves and red fezzes – a gigantic portrait of Rhodes still gazes down with stern approval. Rhodes's resting place on a stunning granite mountain-top in the Matopos Hills is still immaculately cared for, its lonely grandeur desecrated only by huge rainbow lizards of blue-green-orange-yellow basking on his grave in the sun, and the site is still dedicated to 'THOSE WHO HAVE DESERVED WELL OF THEIR COUNTRY.'

But there are small clouds gathering on Zimbabwe's blue horizon. Even those who admire Mugabe's real achievements, in education, health and especially his reconciliation of the tribes and races, fear that he is losing touch with reality and is surrounded by yes-men who tremble to tell him the truth.

'He's a great man,' I was told by his friend Sir Garfield Todd, the one-time white liberal Southern Rhodesian Prime Minister who gave the nineteen-year-old Mugabe his first job as a mission teacher and who sided openly with the black guerrillas during the war. 'But I don't think he's perfect and I'm afraid of his one-party state. Nobody wants it, not even the blacks, and there's a lot of corruption in his Government. People here may begin to think that honesty is a white virtue. I hope he's president for no longer than another five years. Not even an angel should have more than fifteen years in power.'

Official corruption is rampant. There's a ten-year waiting list for new cars because of the restrictions on foreign currency (it can cost £100,000 to acquire a new Mercedes) and several of Mugabe's ministers could not resist the temptation to cash in: a judicial enquiry into vehicle racketeering in 1989 (the Willowgate Scandal) resulted in the resignations of five ministers. One committed suicide.

It is not only extremists like Ian Smith who believe that unless Mugabe abandons his dream of Marxism and inefficient Africanisation, encourages foreign investment and relaxes economic controls and bureaucratic incompetence, the country could slide slowly into the sort of economic shambles that have overtaken the desperate neighbouring states of Zambia and Mozambique. Officially you get four Zimbabwe dollars for £1 sterling, but you can get ten on the black market. 'The rich have got richer and the poor poorer,' I was told often. Domestic staff earn only £8 for a six-day week, shop assistants just £20 a week. Holidays abroad are impossible for most because each resident is allowed to take out of the country just £110 a year. 'We're trapped in Paradise,' said one rich white pensioner.

Zimbabwe's internal telephone system is so bad (and its international one so good) that one Harare woman is said recently to have given up trying to order meat from her butcher by telephone: instead she telephoned her mother in London and asked her to ring the butcher in Harare and place the order for her. Even Sir Garfield Todd admits that unemployment is now at fifty per cent of those available for work, and there are now 300,000 school-leavers a year – but only 8000 or so new jobs. Others are worried about the twenty per cent inflation, the sixty-five per cent tax rate, the lack of foreign currency, spare parts and decent transport, the alarming dependence on foreign aid which might soon be going to Eastern Europe instead of Africa.

Many, including blacks, are concerned about what they see as Mugabe's posturing and growing megalomania. Some blacks call him 'Marco Polo' because he is so often abroad, and ask why he spends so much time jetting around the world playing the international statesman when he ought to be sorting out Zimbabwe's problems. Why does he zoom around Harare in large motorcades, they ask, with lights flashing and sirens blaring, forcing other motorists into the gutter? Why doesn't he keep his bossy and surprisingly rich wife Sally (they call her 'Imelda') under control instead of insisting that she be given the title Amai (Mother of the Nation)? And why should it be a criminal offence to lampoon the president?

Nor is Mugabe doing himself any favours by browbeating the press and television. Their timidity allows all sorts of rumours to flourish precisely because they can't be checked – many of them about him and his wife and all of them outrageous. One recent appalling rumour is that rapes of white women are increasing alarmingly and that Zimbabwe's witchdoctors are telling patients with AIDS that the only cure is to rape a white woman. Stupidly the Government has done nothing to quash the frightened gossip.

Ominously for Mugabe he faces increasing opposition from black students and went so far as to close the university in October after there were riots on campus. And more and more blacks are beginning to deride his pretensions. In Harare's elegant Meikle's Hotel, where they still take tea of an afternoon, I heard a smart group of middle-class blacks openly laughing at him. Who does he think he is, one asked, changing Churchill Road to Robert Mugabe Avenue? When Nelson Mandela visited Harare the previous month Mugabe arranged a 'star rally' that was a thinly attended flop, and his sudden announcement of a 'Mandela holiday' was criticised for costing the country £4 million because he had given no advance warning.

If he can bring himself to modify his ideology then Zimbabwe could have a glittering future. It is still 'the jewel of Africa' – efficient, stylish, not a Third World nation at all. The roads between the main towns are fast, well-kept and empty. Harare is a thriving, vibrant, skyscraper city. The shops are packed with sophisticated goods, the light is clean, the colours bright. Most British visitors would love Zimbabwe, and the prices are absurdly low by our standards: a good meal with wine in a smart hotel costs £5. When I was in Harare the cinemas were screening *Shirley Valentine* and *Dangerous Liaisons*. The people are wonderfully friendly and proud with black dignity. Even the pavement beggars sing.

There seems to be astonishingly little racial bitterness on the part of the blacks. The number of whites has dwindled from 250,000 to 80,000 but those who have remained seem welcome. When I was a boy there were no black pupils at my expensive public school near Bulawayo, Falcon College: now one in five is black, many are prefects, Ndebele is a compulsory language, and on high days and holidays both blacks and whites sing the African liberation anthem *Nkosi Sikelel'i Afrika*. In the bad old days it was common for white children to throw stones at black children and for whites to sneer about 'kaffirs' and 'munts'. But as one white war veteran said: 'We're all

Zimbos now.' Many whites now refer to Mugabe and fellow minister Joshua Nkomo as Bob and Josh, and Mugabe's policy of racial reconciliation is a wonderful example to South Africa. As white ex-senator Denis Norman, now Mugabe's Minister of Transport and National Resources, told me: 'I've enormous respect for him. He's not evil or bigoted and it's no good sitting carping on the sidelines. The whites who've stayed are prepared to make a go of it.'

After just a few days in Zimbabwe I wrote in my diary: 'I've seen the future in Africa, and it works.'

But I am still haunted by my last sad memory of Eagle School. The Zulu Head Girl had no idea that down in the tropical valley there had once been an open-air theatre that had echoed to lines from *Julius Caesar*, *Twelfth Night*, *The Tempest*. The thought excited her. Together with the old black groundsman, Mr Paul, we took sticks and hacked our way down the hillside, through coarse waist-high grass, nettles and thorns, wary of snakes. Deep in the undergrowth beneath our feet, like the ruins of some lost civilisation, like memories of King Solomon's Mines, we could just discern the old stone steps leading down to Shakespeare's grotto, to the Bard in the bush. Could this be some awful portent of Zimbabwe's future – the Ides of Mugabe? And when we reached the spot it was completely overgrown. Gone are the terraced seats, the curved stone stage, the clipped grass, the swimming pool, the poignant strains of *Greensleeves*. All that is left is a silent, brackish pond overhung with monster ferns and creepers. There are ghosts here, and the jungle has returned. O my Malvolio so long ago.

Something coughed in the jungle. 'What's that?' asked the head girl, nervous. 'Baboon?'

It coughed again, hollow, *hoo-hoo*.

Leopard, I thought. There used to be plenty of leopards in these hills. 'Let's go,' I said, as nonchalant as possible. 'There's nothing here for me now.'

CHAPTER 2

BEGINNINGS

NEARLY A CENTURY ago my Scots grandfather Alexander
McDowall cursed and creaked and clanked into the sweat-
stained heart of Central Africa by dusty ox-wagon, trekking for
weeks north from the Cape of Good Hope across the wide
brown plains of the old Transvaal and the sullen fords of the
great grey greasy Limpopo River and into the rich tribal home-
lands of the warlike Matabele, of the Shona and Manica, in search
of a dream. For him and the other intrepid British pioneers, as
they dodged Lobengula's terrifying Matabele impis, and the
Union Jack was raised in Salisbury on 12 September 1890 in the
name of Cecil Rhodes and the Great White Queen, Rhodesia
must have seemed a land of glorious promise.

For me too, even a hundred years later, even in the quiet
antiseptic midnight hum of a Jumbo jet at 37,000 feet, there
was a promise of magic in the smell of Africa. It was my forty-
seventh birthday and in just ten hours I would be back in the
land of my birth at last. In the hour before dawn the overnight
British Airways flight from Heathrow to Harare bumped over
Chad and the Central African Republic, shuddering and creaking in the broiling heat that rises from the equator even at
night like a giant's breath, and I thought with wonder of the
equatorial jungles and swamps teeming in the darkness seven
miles beneath my feet, of lions, elephant, chimpanzees, a
whole continent so long ago abandoned. In one night I was
going back thirty years in time, like my grandfather a hundred
years ago in search of a dream.

*

Harare at 9 a.m. was warm and welcoming, from the seventy-degree Zimbabwean sunshine to the jolly smile of the young black woman immigration officer who looked at my passport and grinned delightedly: 'I wasn't even born when you left Zimbabwe!' Even the Big Brother photograph of Robert Mugabe in the customs hall seemed surprisingly benign. The road into Harare from the airport could almost be anywhere in Africa, and the self-important rows of ceremonial Independence flagpoles on either side of the road suggest that at any moment you may be stopped by drunken soldiers at a military roadblock. But the city itself resembles an English suburb. The Harare telephone directory lists so many English names that it comes as no surprise to see that one of them is M. Howe-Thatcher. My hostess's house has a fireplace, beams and hanging brasses, and her garden glows with roses, herbs, a pond, and her lawn is as closely clipped as any in Surbiton. It could be anywhere in the English Home Counties were it not for the swimming pool and the two African servants (the 'houseboy' and the 'garden boy'). In the guest bathroom there are genteel time-warp copies of *The Lady* from 1987, and downstairs in the gloomy hall a pile of old copies of the *Church Times*.

There is crime in Harare, of course, especially theft, and some drivers remove the rotor arm when parking their cars. Yet there seems to be no fear on the streets, which are immaculately tidy and much cleaner than those of London. The shops are packed with goods, despite occasional shortages of items like sandals or sunhats. If this is the Third World, what does that make Eastern Europe, where the shelves are always empty? Prices are very cheap by British standards. Even at the official exchange rate of Z$4 to the £1 I bought four bottles of wine and twenty-four Castle and Lion beers for just £12. But then wages are very low too: African servants are paid the government minimum wage of £8 a week ('their expectations are so much lower than ours,' I was told by one white) and for that they work a nine-hour day, sometimes more, and are allowed only one day a week off. Despite all the hopes and expectations of black independence, the average African

13

doesn't seem to be much better off now than he was under Ian Smith. Even computer programmers with A-levels are paid no more than £40 a week. One of the reasons for the low pay, of course, is the dizzily high level of unemployment.

Torrential rain falls in glittering sheets after lunch, closing the grey sky as it has every afternoon for the last six weeks: not a good omen for my trip, yet the smell of warm, damp tropical earth is irresistible, lingering like perfume in the soporific thrumming of an African thunderstorm until a siesta becomes inevitable. The storm does not last long: by 4.30 the sky has cleared, and in the dusk cheerful African voices colour the wide, tree-lined avenues with happiness, the broad boulevards splashed with the colours of red flamboyant umbrella trees and the blue-mauve jacaranda. Outside Meikle's Hotel are stalls selling huge bunches of glorious flowers. Harare is a haven, a wonderful oasis: clean, elegant, efficient; a thriving, vibrant city far more stylish than most English towns.

Equally cheery in the evening is Ian Smith, the former Rhodesian rebel leader, when I telephone him at his house in the ridiculously English suburb of Belgravia. It seems proper that I should speak to him on my first night back after thirty years: after all, it were his politics, his Unilateral Declaration of Independence, and his war that kept me away for so long. The line echoes and fades and Smith announces cheerfully that it is tapped by Mugabe's secret police. It is uncanny to hear those clipped tones with the narrow vowels that became so familiar in Britain in the 1960s after Smith declared Rhodesia independent and was accused of treason. He is extremely approachable and agrees to an interview soon.

The evening news on Zimbabwean TV is riveting, mainly because the black newsreader is so nervous he looks as though he expects to be hanged at dawn himself if he gets something wrong or deviates from the Party line. Every black man he mentions is described as 'Comrade' but every white man is plain 'Mister'. This is obviously Zimbabwe's new racial discrimination: these days you have to be black to be taken as Red. The newsreader's eyes flicker. Is some sadistic camera-

14

man making faces at him? His wispy little beard twitches. He speaks in a tortuously correct 1950s Oxford accent, the like of which is rarely heard in Britain today. He reports that three politicians in Nepal have been placed under house arrest for urging a return to a multi-party state. Nepal? Can Zimbabweans in the Zambezi Valley or the mountains of the Vumba really have any interest in what goes on in Nepal? Of course not: but it's useful propaganda when you remember that Comrade President Mugabe is also trying to denigrate the virtues of democracy and to praise the advantages of a one-party state. Yet a moment later our newsreader delivers a sudden nervous item of news about that most democratic of games, cricket, because the England A team is touring Zimbabwe, which hopes the tour will be so successful that it will be recognised as a cricketing country of full Test status. Somehow cricket and one-party states don't seem to go together at all. What other independent, black, Marxist, one-party dictatorship dreams of appearing in Wisden?

The jumpy TV newsreader, who seems now to be under the impression that somebody is creeping up behind him, proceeds to report hurriedly some exceedingly dull developments in Albania and Yugoslavia. Then at last there are items of local news: a new clean-water project out in the bush; and the primary polls for candidates in the Zimbabwean general election – all of them, of course, from Mugabe's ruling ZANU-PF party, which would doubtless gratify the King of Nepal. The screen pulsates with pictures of fat African women dancing and stamping and ululating.

Later another unlikely programme warns of the dangers of smoking, even though tobacco is Zimbabwe's major crop and one if its few foreign currency earners. This seems morally admirable but economically crazy. Surely Zimbabwe should be *encouraging* smoking to keep its economy alight. When I was a boy forty years ago smoking was patriotic here, and you could buy cigarettes (cynically called Long Life) in packs of fifty for just half a crown (12½p).

*

My hostess becomes as jittery as the newsreader when I'm still trying to make telephone calls after 9 p.m., even though it's a Saturday night. 'We never ring anyone after 8.45,' she says, 'because we all get up at 5.30.' Even on Sunday? Yes.

Early to bed then, and up at 6.15 a.m. for church. I wake to the nostalgic sound of African voices in the street outside my window, brash free African voices chuckling in colonialist Rhodes Avenue. There is also the soft cooing of pigeons, so that I wake bewildered, imagining I am back in my old eighteenth-century thatched cottage on the Berkshire downs with the honeysuckle crawling up the brick and flint walls and the wild pigeons calling from the vast octagonal dovecote built by monks in 1652. But Zimbabwean pigeons sound more breathless than English ones and as throaty and nervous as any Zimbabwean newsreader. The sky is a pale eggshell blue, the light clean and bright, the palm trees glistening in the morning dew. There is a lovely fresh smell, and the trill of an African whistling happily outside.

There are seventy worshippers at the 7.30 communion ser-vice in the Anglican cathedral, twenty of them black. The black priest, in startlingly bright green vestments, speaks thickly incomprehensible English but drones on and on in a mono-tone worthy of the dreariest English village vicar. Two white women stand beside him at attention by the altar, serving wine, ecclesiastical barmaids. The black and white reversal of roles since independence is striking: the European women are stiff, subservient acolytes and one of them, white-haired and beak-nosed, could be an ageing virgin priestess at some pagan ceremony. Later on a platform in the belltower we watch the white bellringers tugging at their ropes and sending the clang of English religion echoing across this tribal Shona city in the heart of the ancient empire of the legendary chieftain Munhumutapa, who is said to have built a very different sort of temple at Great Zimbabwe.

Around the cathedral's inside walls there are garish African murals, the Stations of the Cross, a strikingly negroid Christ with negroid Roman soldiers. But embedded too in the walls

16

nearby are plaques commemorating worthy old white Rhodesian colonialists and pioneers, pale heroes of the British South Africa Police (also founded a hundred years ago) and the arrogant imperialists who crushed Lobengula in 1893 and the Matabele Rebellion in 1896. You would think that such colonial memorials would be anathema to Mugabe and his people, but in the tranquil cloisters outside there is also a chapel with plaques remembering the white civilian passengers who died in the two Viscount airliners shot down by Joshua Nkomo's ZAPU guerrillas in 1978 and 1979. In the leafy square beside the cathedral – once Cecil Square in honour of Cecil Rhodes, now African Unity Square – the colourful tropical trees and plants and flowers are still arranged around the paths in an unforgettably British shape. Photographed from above they would look, as they always have, like the Union Jack.

Breakfast couldn't be more English – egg, bacon and sausage – and then six of us drive thirty miles out of Harare, on a beautiful African day, through the lush green countryside along avenues of blue gum trees, to meet two friends for lunch at Marondera, an idyllic spot, amazingly green after the recent rains. We eat at the Malwatti Tea Rooms, a smart bungalow restaurant where we take a table for eight in the sun on the lawn under the trees. Nothing seems to have changed since Ian Smith was running the country. There's hardly a black face in sight except for the polite and friendly waiters in their crisp white uniforms and a few of the black boys from the smart local public school, Peterhouse, out for the day with their parents and looking hot and uncomfortable in their absurd English-style uniforms: long grey flannel trousers, blazers, ties. The place appears to be the essence of modern Zimbabwe: it's *suburban*; Woking in the sun, with bougainvillea. On the road here from Harare, even in the rural wilds, the verges are clipped tidy and the road is smoother and better maintained than many rural roads in Britain. At lunch a woman at the next table announces loudly to her friends: 'Tracksuits are all the rage in London now, you know. Everyone wears them, men and women.' Ancient fashions are still hot news in Zimbabwe.

Lunch is amazingly cheap: just £30 for eight of us to eat remarkably well on excellent steak or chicken, salad, chips, apple pie, three bottles of very drinkable local wine; in all less than £4 each. My guests think this is dreadfully expensive, and indeed it is in local terms: a teacher starting his career at Peterhouse, a prime public boarding school, is paid only £3000 a year and the boys' fees are only £600 a term. 'We're allowed to take only £100 a year in cash out of the country,' says one of my guests, 'and just £250 if a whole family emigrates. So UK prices are terrifying. Forex is a magic word here.'

Forex = foreign exchange.

On the road back to Harare the buses and lorries belch clouds of fumes so thick that visibility is almost nil. Spare parts are rare because of the shortage of foreign currency, and although Mugabe has recently gone fashionably Green, and pledged himself to preserve the environment, Zimbabwe's buses and lorries must be doing as much damage to the ozone layer as an entire British motorway.

In Harare, near Mugabe's presidential palace, we suddenly screech off the road and brake hard as a motorcade hurtles past with flashing lights, blaring sirens and a police convoy. This is how Comrade President Mugabe travels about his capital city, and any motorist who doesn't get out of the way damned quick is likely to be gunned down or arrested. It's said that two motorists have already been shot and killed for not reacting quickly enough. Apparently Mugabe is terrified of assassination and the gossip is that there have already been six attempts on his life, all of them by disgruntled blacks. The outer walls of his palace are patrolled constantly by armed guards and in the streets round about there is a shoot-to-kill curfew from 6 p.m. to 6 a.m. Rumour has it that there is a helicopter on permanent standby in the palace grounds to allow Mugabe to make a fast getaway if there's ever a coup – a real possibility as increasing numbers of Africans become disillusioned with his regime and accuse him of failing to deliver, of selling out to the whites and breaking his promises to them.

A swim in the pool in the afternoon, and then the nightly excitement of the ZBC-TV news, presented this time by a hard-faced white woman newsreader with a gritty voice and a puzzled expression. She reports on the primary election nominations and still calls everyone 'Comrade' but manages brilliantly to pronounce the inverted commas. She regales her tribal viewers in the distant reaches of the Zambezi valley with news of San Salvador. There are two TV channels and they screen programmes like *Dallas* and (from Britain) *This Week*. One radio favourite is *My Word!* with Frank Muir and Denis Norden. It also seems that almost every European here reads the English *Sunday Telegraph* (a few days later, of course) 'because it's a good right-wing paper.'

It's easy to pick up good habits in Harare when everyone goes to bed at 9 p.m., and again on Monday morning I wake at five to the cooing of doves. At 5.30 the traffic is already chuntering along Rhodes Avenue and a golden dawn comes up, the sky the colour of paw-paw. The light is wonderfully clean.

Laurie Sparham has turned up – my photographer from London – and we pick up a hire car from Hertz and set off at last towards Mutare, my birthplace. It's thirty years since I travelled this road but the route is as familiar as yesterday: gigantic outcrops of granite rearing above the bush; huge rocks impossibly balanced one on another like children's teetering building blocks; one remembered mountain rising smooth and steep out of the landscape like a vast grey volcanic whale surfacing from the sea. But nowadays the road is smooth and fast and beautifully maintained and not just the two thin strips of tar that it once was. There are very few potholes – not nearly as many as in the First World London boroughs of Fulham and Southwark. As we approach the Mozambique border we pass two Zimbabwean armoured trucks lumbering east towards some jungle battle with the Renamo terrorists across the border, where the Zimbabwean army is helping Mozambican government troops.

It's so hot and sticky that my copper anti-rheumatism bracelet has dyed the skin of my wrist a dark dirty green, but on the final mountainous approach to Mutare the road over Christmas Pass gleams with recent rain. The view from the pass of the spreading circular plain of Mutare far below is breathtaking, the town a tiny toy glistening in the distance. Here one misty Christmas in the 1890s my grandfather and the horseback British pioneers first gazed with awe on the plain beneath, the tribal homeland of the Manica chieftain King Mtasa. But before long the horizon would become black with the silhouettes of the 'nodding donkeys' of the Penhalonga gold mines, and white diggers from the Rezende Mine (perhaps one of King Solomon's) would jog their mules down this mountainside with bags of gold dust stitched to their saddles like Butch Cassidy and the Sundance Kid, nervous of bandits, down the hill to the first Standard Bank, where my grandfather was a chartered accountant and maybe knew the pretty but dangerous British nurse who was engaged six times in Umtali in the 1890s but whose six fiancés all died within weeks (of blackwater fever) before she could coax them to the altar. And down there in the plain, three years after my grandfather died in 1940, I was born (clubfooted, like the Devil and Byron) in one of those distant dinky buildings – in the Lady Kennedy Nursing Home – as close then in time to the pioneers as to 1990, halfway between the beginning and now.

Down the mountain we drive, down into Umtali-Mutare, along Main Street, still the wide one-horse Wild West thoroughfare I loved so well, and I imagine the silent voices of my ancestors calling me home. My whiskered Victorian grandfather drove his governess cart along this street nearly a century ago, with a pretty white pony called Molly, and once owned all that land, there, where the convent school stands; and my lovely mother (dead now for twenty-four years) was born here too, in one of the airy side-street verandah houses there on the left, down Sixth Avenue; and my beloved Aunt

Dolly, who now lives in Oxford, was born here eighty-four years ago, only yards away behind the avenue of red flamboyant trees that Cecil Rhodes paid for himself; and the neat white colonial police station still looks pink in the twilight, as tasty as coconut ice. My beautiful, fragile grandmother, who died so young, at twenty-seven, lies in the cemetery along that road on the right, and there are mute ghosts too in the centre of town haunting the derelict site where the elegant old Cecil Hotel once stood, its wide white porticoed verandah tinkling with colonial small talk and iced drinks, its airy fan-cooled dining room rich with the odours of roast beef and Yorkshire pudding and African waiters sweating in black bow-ties and white gloves. For years my grandfather managed the finances of the Cecil Hotel and Rhodes himself used to tether his horse to the hitching rail outside.

Today it has all gone, demolished without trace except for a few faded floor tiles as red and sullen as sunburn beneath the belligerent weeds. No grandeur is left, no Sunday afternoon dreams, just empty cigarette packets and pork pie wrappings tossed among the nettles. Beside the overgrown site of the Cecil Hotel stands its bland rectangular red-brick replacement, the Manica, a sort of giant's lunchbox, the kind of faceless modern rent-a-bed hotel that you will find in any town in any continent. The Manica has television sets in every room and 'hygienically cleaned' plastic wrappers on the lavatory seats, and printed lavatory paper so twee and genteel it would surely blush at the mention of shit. The usual Big Brother portrait of Robert Mugabe peers down benignly from behind the reception desk and from vantage points in every store and supermarket, though the more I see it the more I think of it as Little Brother: Mugabe seems like a ghost who is everywhere and yet nowhere at all.

The town is amazingly clean and neat, the First World War memorial spruce and lovingly tended in its colourful gardens. There are hardly any white faces on the bustling streets any more, but the black schoolchildren from Mutare High School look smart and the African adults are courteous and friendly,

21

even the drunks lurching outside the bars at 4 p.m. There is only one beggar, a woman with two small children, sitting on the pavement outside Meikle's department store, and she is singing. There are shortages of cars, spare parts, and goods like Marmite and films, and Kingston's bookshop has hardly any hardbacks for sale, but under the 'African Writers' section there is a copy of *The Importance of Being Earnest* by that well-known black humorist Oscar Wilde. But other stores are packed with video tapes, jewellery, three-piece suites, whisky at £10 a bottle (expensive for a Zimbabwean, the equivalent of £40 a bottle). Meikle's department store (also once managed by my grandfather) still sells English-style school uniforms, and at OK Bazaars a pair of khaki shorts costs £1.25, and I buy a green sunhat for £1. OK Bazaars! What sticky boyhood memories loiter in the name alone.

Some things, though, haven't changed. The Mutare Club, a quaint one-storey building, still skulks behind verandahs with white wooden balustrades beneath an odd octagonal pep-perpot tower with a slate-grey roof. Outside on the pavement, staunch and squat, is a red Southern Rhodesian colonial post-box still marked SR GPO. The club has 350 members and it seems that every one of them is white. The walls are adorned with old colonial photographs and the members still talk today in the slang of old Rhodesia, of 'tickies' (threepence) and 'tack-ies' (tennis shoes), and they still wear the old Rhodesian uniform of khaki shorts and open-necked shirts. My boozy, clubbable grandfather, who became one of Umtali's first town councillors and owned the large house opposite the club, would hardly notice a difference today. In the bar, beside a bulldog portrait of Winston Churchill, his name gleams in golden letters on the wooden honours board listing past chairmen of the club: 1920, A. McDowall. His house across the road, number 115 – a prosperous whitewashed bungalow with a wide verandah, chunky colonnade of white pillars, black tin roof and net curtains as coy as any English suburb – is now the unlikely headquarters of the local Anglican Church, the office of the Diocese of Manicaland, which would have made him laugh: he was not a religious man.

It would be easy to be depressed by the Mutare Club, for it seems to be just as racist and white-supremacist as it always was. Back at the new Manica Hotel the atmosphere is very different, yet oddly exclusive in its own way. The Railway Bar is packed with thirty Africans immaculately dressed in ties and jackets, despite the heat, and I, the only white, am asked by the African barman to leave because I am not wearing a tie. I have left all mine by mistake in Harare and have to borrow, a skinny blue-and-pink monstrosity from the reception desk. The bar is adorned with old Rhodesian Railways signs saying 'Tickets' and 'Waiting Room', with the page of a newspaper dated 1900, and with old train timetables where the colonial names of Salisbury, Umtali and Marandellas have been altered roughly to read Harare, Mutare, Marondera. They look crude, almost childish, and there is something touching about the independent Africans' determination to assert their freedom and yet cling to the bourgeois trappings of collars, ties and British historical relics. They have kept, too, an inimitably *African* brand of logic. When I try to telephone England to speak to Aunt Dolly, who hasn't seen the town for thirty-five years, I have to place the call through the hotel switchboard and there are continual delays and misunderstandings over the number and the code for England. 'Ah,' says the black operator eventually, with sudden wondrous understanding. 'You wish to call England *in particular*.'

Laurie and I drive back up Christmas Pass for dinner at the Wise Owl with old friends of mine, and again I'm astonished by the low prices here. A round of drinks and a three-course dinner for six with two bottles of wine, coffee and brandy, comes to £35, including the tip, less than a smart meal for one in London now. Nor is the Wise Owl some cheap hamburger joint: at the next table are the England A cricket team, about to play a three-day match in Mutare.

At midnight in my room in the Manica Hotel, in a self-indulgent moment of nostalgic research, I am reading the first chapter of my old novel about Africa, *The Nostradamus Horo-scope*, which includes the first verse of the anthem *God Bless Africa*, when suddenly I hear the same anthem belting out from the TV across the corridor as ZBC closes down its trans-missions for the night:

> *Ishe komberera Africa!*
> *Ngaisimvdzirwe zita rayo*
> *Inzwai miteuro yedu*
> *Isu mhuri yayo.*

['God bless Africa! Let its name be uplifted. Hear our prayers, we the children of Africa.']

The old town clock strikes twelve, the clock whose chimes were heard by my white forefathers and measured their lives and deaths and also struck the hour of midnight a few minutes before I was born. South of the border, across the great grey Limpopo River, the hope of black South Africa, Nelson Mandela, has just been liberated from prison to begin a new day in history.

As I drift into sleep, with the black night quiet in the place of my birth, I marvel at the dignity of black Zimbabweans today, a dignity they were denied for so long by my own white tribe. I think of the black barman who asked me politely to leave because I was wearing no tie, of the black school-children, straight and confident, whose own forefathers were not much better than slaves. This used to be called God's Own Country, and it is. I've fallen in love with it all over again.

At 6 a.m. the burnished sun comes up suddenly over Mutare from out of a pale Mozambican dawn behind Cross Kopje, rising fast like a huge white balloon above the towering cruci-fix that was raised on the summit of the hill to honour the dead of the First World War. As the sun melts the steaming mist in the rills and valleys of the Vumba foothills, I gaze out of my hotel window at this day of which I have dreamed for thirty years. The air tastes crisp and the silent avenues lie wide and fresh beneath the scarlet blossoms of the very flamboyant trees that Cecil Rhodes had planted here (and paid for himself) when he ordered Old Umtali to be moved up and over the mountain from the other side of Christmas Pass. Scattered before me in the white morning are pale bungalows with red roofs, wooded gardens, palm trees, a weathercock nesting high on the narrow spire of a church. Already the sky is deep blue and the warmth enough to tingle the skin. My spirits lift as quickly as the sun. My birthplace, the Lady Kennedy Nursing Home on Murambi Drive, overlooking the Hillside golf course, is now an old folks' home and so nowadays a place of frequent death, too. But I'm glad I was born here. It's a place of bright, clean light and colour, a good place to be born and better than most for dying.

CHAPTER 3

YOUNG EAGLES AT LEOPARD ROCK

HIGH IN THE Vumba Mountains above Mutare, 5000 feet above sea level, where the mist is as fresh as the dew of the highlands of Scotland, there nestles secretly amid the lush greenery of the eastern edge of Zimbabwe a fantastical fairytale palace, complete with towers and turrets, that flirts with the dangerous Mozambique border with the hidden menace of a childhood horror story by the Brothers Grimm. It even has its own gloomy lake, and magical queen, and legendary princess. It is the old Leopard Rock Hotel, long derelict but about to open again, where the Queen Mother and Princess Margaret stayed for several nights during their tour of Rhodesia in 1953 – and the African caretaker, who was then the wine waiter, still remembers vividly how close he came then to the Great White Queen from across the seas.

The advice from the British High Commission in Harare is to keep well clear of this border area because of the recent increase in the activities of the Mozambican guerrillas, who have just kidnapped two white men not so far away. But these beautiful mountains are where I spent eight years of my childhood, just a few miles down the road, as a boarder at Eagle prep school from the ages of six to thirteen, and Leopard Rock was where our parents took us on our rare Sunday exeats in the 1940s and 1950s and treated us to lunch and tea. It would take an even greater coward than I to keep away now.

Laurie Sparham and I drove up into the silent blue mountains through soft damp woods, along quiet lanes smelling of earth. In the spring, in September, these msasa trees gleam with polished gold and pink. The mild Vumba air was balmy and it was the sun, not a gang of Renamo guerrillas, that streamed across the valley from Mozambique. Leopard Rock is perched on the edge of the Mozambique border and has stunning views over the haze of savannah towards the Indian Ocean 170 miles away. The hotel is tucked away at the end of a secret leafy driveway and has three pointy fairytale towers, a wicked-stepmother castle, and the vast hanging rock itself looming over all. Lawns stretch down to a stagnant lake and an abandoned ivy-covered hut where we used to take afternoon tea and scones and fairy cakes.

All is hushed in the sunlight, as still as the memories of the imperial dreamers who built the place, and it is easy to imagine knights and dragons beside the mirrored lake and a princess in one of the towers pining for her lover, yearning from an upper casement, her tresses cascading down stone walls. So it seems appropriate that it was in this remote fortress, in the middle tower, that twenty-two-year-old Princess Margaret stayed for three days in June 1953, rude and sulky so they say, lonely and lovesick, telephoning Group Captain Peter Townsend in England night after night, the landline from Leopard Rock to London fading and booming and echoing across thousands of miles of jungle and desert while the Queen Mother occupied the right-hand tower and smiled and smiled and smiled. When the Queen Mum visited us at Eagle School at the end of that stay there was no sign of the promised princess. She was probably on the telephone.

Leopard Rock has been a place of hatred and violence as well as love. It was a dangerous spot during the war of black independence, when Robert Mugabe's terrorists were launching murderous attacks on Ian Smith's Rhodesia from their camps just across the Mozambique border. The hotel's outer walls are still pockmarked with bullet holes, and it has long been deserted. But it is being refurbished by its new owner, Patrick Honey, an Eagle contemporary of mine who hopes to open it again as hotel and casino in 1991, and the gardens are once again trim and ablaze with tropical colour. The hotel is empty except for the gardener and the small, wiry, white-haired caretaker, 'Mr Damson' (Damson Muzhange) who wears a bright floral jacket (with a delicate pink rose motif) made out of an old curtain. He was wine waiter here until 1974 and then head waiter until 1984, when the hotel was closed for lack of business, and he is still touchingly eager to talk about its history. He shows us proudly to the tower rooms where the royals slept nearly forty years ago and woke to breathtaking views across the dewy lawns below and the purple Portuguese plains stretching towards the Indian Ocean. In what was once the Queen Mother's bathroom there is still a lavatory-roll holder, but otherwise the royal rooms are dere-lict and echoing, the floorboards bare, the paint peeling and discoloured, the walls cracked, the electrical fittings torn out, their wires dangling loose. The baths that once caressed the royal flesh are stained with rust. Mr Damson says there are no ghosts here, but there ought to be, for these regal rooms smell of rot and sadness. Downstairs, where one wall of the dining room is a vast rock jutting out of the mountainside, the empty bar still has on the counter a card showing the prices of drinks in 1984. In the snooker room the trophies of animal heads have all been removed, leaving patches on the walls as pale as spectres.

And then there's the gloomy children's playroom, where the tiniest Eagles, aged six or seven, would spend the occasional Sunday afternoon hour desperately pretending to forget that all too soon it would be back to school and the brief departing smell of mother's powdered cheeks, and those hot, shameful tears of goodbye, and the dreary evening service melancholy with the strains of *Abide With Me*, and that tomorrow it would be Latin again, and prep, for ever and ever, Amen. I had forgot-ten how dark and threatening the children's playroom was, but now it envelopes Laurie and Mr Damson and me like a nightmare, a hollow dungeon with a large grey model castle and garish murals of Snow White and the Seven Dwarfs, and Goofy, and a medieval scene with a knight in armour waiting to rescue the princess in the tower. Only now the princess is long gone, many thousands of miles away across jungle and desert, with her youth and love, her loneliness and longing. Her old upper room in the central tower glistens with cobwebs and echoes only the tiptoes of spiders. Even in the tropics it is possible to shiver.

A few miles down the road Eagle School is another extraordinary place haunted by love, hate, imperial history and nightmare. It was founded in 1948 by Frank Cary and other masters from the Dragon School, Oxford, where Harold Pinter's wife Lady Antonia Fraser was a pupil and played rugby as a girl. Eagle squats on a ledge overlooking the Burma Valley, nine miles above Mutare and five from the Mozambique border, surrounded by savage but beautiful granite mountains: Castle Beacon, The Saddle, Camel's Hump, names that conjure up a multitude of memories. For thirty years it was an oasis of private English educational excellence in these wild highlands.

Laurie is obviously baffled by my feeling for this place, which I suppose is almost an obsession. I can see him thinking: come *on*, it was only a *school*, for Krissake. Yet I am not alone among the many boys who were lucky enough to be boarders there and remember it with unusual warmth and gratitude. Indeed, one of the school's four headmasters, Frank Cary's successor, Claude Mellor, inspired such affection and respect that even now, at the age of eighty, retired though he is in the Isle of Man, he still receives regular letters from dozens of us and travels the world to visit his old pupils and stay with them.

But the gentle story of Eagle is also spattered with blood. On the terrible night of Friday 23 June 1978, during the black war of independence, black guerrillas did indeed creep across the border from Mozambique, slinking west in the darkness past Leopard Rock and along the valley and up to the school. There, in circumstances of inconceivable savagery, they slaughtered the white teachers and their wives and children – thirteen of them. The females were all sexually assaulted. The victims were beaten with logs and stabbed and one woman

29

was found with an axe buried deep in her shoulder. The massacre took place at 8.30 p.m. on the path beside the sports
pavilion (now the tuckshop) 500 feet from the school.

Responsibility for this horror is still disputed. One senior
white politician who was close to Ian Smith during the years
of UDI and civil war told me that he thinks it just possible
that the atrocity was in fact committed not by Mugabe's
ZANLA terrorists (nor by the supporters of the Rev Ndaban-
ingi Sithole, who have also been blamed) but by Ian Smith's
white Selous Scouts security forces ('there were some hard
bastards there') as a piece of ruthless black disinformation
propaganda. But Smith himself denied it vociferously when
I asked him in Harare, and the then Rector of St John's
church in Mutare, John Knight, who carried the coffin of
the smallest victim at the mass funeral, claims in his book
Rain in a Dry Land not only that the slaughter was indeed
carried out by a gang of seventeen young black 'freedom
fighters' but that nine of them later repented of their sin
and were converted to Christianity, and that the leader of
the gang, 'Gavin', is now a born-again evangelist in Zambia.
Mr Knight seems to derive some weird satisfaction from this
story, especially from the possibility that thirteen whites
(including four small children) were martyred so that nine
black men might be 'born again'.

I have already described that foul night in Chapter 1 and it
is pointless to linger on it – except perhaps to list the names
of the victims, simple unarmed missionary teachers of the Elim
Pentecostal Mission and their wives and babies, whose names
now appear to be recorded only in the fusty cuttings library
of the *Herald* newspaper in Harare. They were Peter McCann
(30), his wife Sandra (30), and children Philip (6) and Joy
(5); the Reverend Philip Evans (29), his wife Susan (35) and
daughter Rebecca (4); Roy Lynn (37), his wife Joyce (36) and
daughter Pamela (3 weeks); and Catherine Picken (55), Eliza-
beth Hamilton-White (37), and Mary Fisher (28) who somehow
survived the night and was found the next day in some bushes
but died a few days later in hospital. One missionary survived

– Ian McGarrick, who was working in his room throughout the massacre and heard nothing.

For anyone who was raised at Eagle a return visit is bound to be coloured by dark memories of that slaughter. For years I had dreamed of Eagle, both before and after the massacre, and even when I was forty-one the place was still so embedded in my psyche that I based an entire chapter on it in my 1986 novel, *Time Out of Mind*, which is also set (by odd coincidence) thirty years later. In the book the school appears as both a school and a medieval monastery violated by a brutal barbarian rabble, and I imagined in that chapter how it might be now, after the horror and now that it had been turned by the Mugabe Government into a military training centre. In the novel I wrote:

> Did the spirits of their terrified victims still haunt the school quad where the invaders had corralled them, or the football pitch where the headmaster and his staff had been killed? In the early evening, as the tropical sun died swiftly in a blaze of garish changing colour, I sensed in the heavy silence of the corridors a presence of unseen shadows and unheard screams, and I shivered with the chill feeling of fading ancient memories and the damp monastic must of the chapel at night. Behind it was a mass grave where the guerrillas had dumped the bodies. It was marked now by a simple white stone engraved with more than a dozen names and the line 'Requiescat in Pace'. I stood before it one evening with bowed head and prayed that they were indeed at peace, that it was only my imagination that sensed them flitting with horror and bewilderment through classrooms and dormitories filled with men of a colour always to haunt them in their restless eternities. Can the dead be haunted by the living? Are there ghosts from the future as well as from the past?

When Auberon Waugh reviewed the novel with his usual alarming insight (in the *Daily Mail*) he sensed that this chapter had been dredged from some appalling depth and even mentioned the massacre at Eagle without knowing that I had been to school there: so my return stirred old apprehension. Would shadows flit in sudden corners where once we played hop-scotch or clicked our marbles or swopped comics and catapults? Would there indeed be places – by Top Gate per-haps, or on Bottom Field – where no birds sing?

In fact Eagle School today is nothing like a military camp. There is no mass grave, as I had imagined, nor any white stone marked 'Requiescat in Pace'. In the school grounds there is not even any memorial at all. It was not until the very end of my pilgrimage that I discovered that the victims of that horrific night in 1978 have not been completely forgotten.

My return to Eagle resurrected another murky memory, one so personal and grubby that I still marvel at my deep affection for the school. It is the sort of memory that should have made me hate the place, yet I don't. When I was seven or eight I was sexually assaulted more than once at Eagle by the school's founder, my first headmaster, Frank Cary, who must then have been in his forties. I was not his only victim, and the experience was embarrassing and baffling rather than distressing.

'Tank' Cary was a tall, skinny man with a weird weakness for very small boys. He would come to some of us in our dormitories after lights-out and sit on our narrow monastic beds in the dark, muttering about Dirty Habits and sliding his hand under the bedclothes to fiddle optimistically with our minuscule 'private parts' (as they were known then) while we lay carefully at attention, rather astonished. Boys of seven or eight, of course, cannot imagine that their headmaster is cap-able of doing wrong, so none of us dreamed of complaining about Cary's attentions, which dwindled once we reached the geriatric age of nine. But in 1956, by which time 'Tank' had moved on to found my future public school near Bulawayo, and I was thirteen and had long forgotten the episode, one of his victims complained and the police were called in. Detec-tives arrived at Eagle, where I was now School Captain, and eventually I was one of nine boys who had to give evidence against 'Tank' in Bulawayo Magistrates Court. I was astonished to see who the other eight witnesses were – and depressed, too, to see how ugly they all were.

The trial dragged on for five appalling, shameful days, from 16–20 October 1956, attracting front-page headlines in the *Sunday Mail* of 21 October, and Cary was sent to prison for a year on the day that the Russians marched into Poland and it was announced that Roy Welensky was succeeding Lord Malvern as Prime Minister of the Central African Federation.

Frank Cary's conviction was a tragic end to the career of a distinguished teacher (a married man with daughters) who had come out to Africa from Oxford to found not only Rhodesia's best prep school, Eagle, but also its best public school, Falcon College. He died, broken, not many years after his release from prison.

Should I feel guilty for having given evidence against 'Tank' Cary? No, of course not: it is indefensible for a headmaster to fiddle with his pupils, some of us hardly more than infants, and it was deeply unpleasant to have to give the most intimate evidence against him in open court at the age of thirteen and to be questioned at length with ruthless scepticism by his counsel while my daunting old headmaster sat just feet in front of me, staring at me, and my father listened appalled at the back of the court. At one stage during my cross-examination I sobbed with shame and embarrassment, and needed a glass of water. But 'Tank' was not an evil man, and I was left with no psychological scars or bitterness. A month later I was even able to sit (and win) the Falcon College scholarship exam, despite the distraction of the court case, and to go on to Falcon three months after I had helped to send its headmaster to jail. Perhaps children are more resilient than the recent hysteria in Britain over child abuse would suggest: certainly I suffered much more from the attentions of the police and the lawyers than I had ever done from the attentions of Cary; the trial itself was undoubtedly child abuse. But it still seems astonishing that a headmaster with so much to lose should have risked and lost everything for a few brief fumblings with little boys

33

in open dormitories. Just three years after Frank Cary was introducing the Queen Mother to his Eagle School boys and staff he was in prison. Poor desperate man. His wife and daughters must have suffered much more than I did, and they must have hated me afterwards. *Requiescat* Frank Cary, too – a victim also of a terrible civil war, his own, that eventually destroyed him as surely as if he had been massacred by terrorists.

Before making that long-imagined pilgrimage back to Eagle School I tracked down its last headmaster, Michael Hammond (ex-Dragon School, Oxford, of course). Today he teaches at Marondera, at Peterhouse, one of Zimbabwe's few posh public schools. He was headmaster of Eagle from 1973 to 1976, when there were bombs exploding in the African village in the valley below and he and the governors suddenly decided that it was too dangerous to stay on in such a remote spot so close to the Mozambique border and the terrorists. They abandoned the school immediately, in the middle of the holidays, and moved the one hundred boys to Springvale School at Marondera the next term. Eagle was sold to the missionaries, even though they were warned of the dangers and Michael Hammond returned to warn them again just three weeks before the massacre. They were planning to move out – but too late. Hammond has kept the old Eagle School honours boards in a room at Springvale, where he and his wife Barry now live in the girls' part of Peterhouse. It's startlingly green after the recent rains, and the girls are spruce in khaki uniforms. Springvale's Picture Room is a place of absurd nostalgia for me, for here are all the relics that were saved when Eagle was abandoned in 1976: the honours boards, the silver cups, old team photographs. To see the name of just one trophy, the Quentin Skene Cup, brings back a torrent of memories, and there on three of the honours boards, preserved in gold lettering, is my name under the year 1956, when I was thirteen: School Captain, Gold Medal, Scholarship. Such small triumphs, so pathetically cherished. I am dazed by crowded thoughts of long ago and by all those forgotten names on all those honours boards: Mike Honey, Brian Bowles, Peter Beaumont, Mike Jamieson, Gilly Cottrell, Andrew Moncreiff. Once I expected all of us to be famous.

On a magical sunny morning in February Laurie and I set off from Mutare at 9 a.m. to drive up the Vumba to Eagle. The road seems as familiar as yesterday, an idyllic route into the mountains, through forests of gum trees with glorious views to the east over Mozambique, where maybe only a few hundred yards away the Renamo rebels roam, where somewhere in the bush the kidnapped men perhaps lie terrified, wondering if maybe this is to be their last day.

After eight miles we reach Top Gate, where we lined up to be inspected by the Queen Mother and Frank Cary. We swing the car down the bumpy red earth track towards the school, through Fourth Forest, Third Forest, Second Forest, First Forest, sniffing the dank richness of trees and wet Vumba bracken in these hills where our teachers sometimes went out at dawn with shotguns (and one with a bow and arrow) to hunt marauding leopard, through the dark, festering forests with trickling mountain streams and trailing monkey-ropes on which we swung like tiny Tarzans.

The school gate now is a black-and-white striped pole, like a customs barrier. Beside it is a sign that reads MINISTRY OF STATE, Political Affairs, EAGLE TRAINING CENTRE. Can the rumour really be true, that Eagle is not the civil service secretarial college it pretends to be but is in fact now a secret training centre for Zimbabwean Mata Hari women spies? It seems unlikely. Nothing much seems to be secret here. The chubby black security woman 'guarding' the gate, Irene Makarahwa, is friendly and chides me for arriving late. 'We were expecting you yesterday,' she beams. She seems a most unlikely security guard for a top-secret spy school and could quite easily be running the bric-a-brac stall at an English village fête, with her crisp white pleated skirt and vast breasts sagging low in a blue woolly sweater. Almost certainly she has no idea at all that just over her shoulder, just there on the right, mass murder was committed one brutal night twelve years ago in the blameless shin-deep grass of the quiet, cool little glade beside the red-roofed sports pavilion, just yards from the hockey goalposts and the cricket scoreboard where the black-and-white metal numberplates in the umbrella shadow of a spreading tree still read unconvincingly Last Man 268, 1st Innings 466. Last man 268? The girls here now must be better at cricket than we were. Could these very numbers have been the doomed missionaries' last earthly sight as they tried to sing hymns beside the pavilion while they were hacked to death with axes and knives on their final bloody night? Last Man 268? Was that the last thing they saw? 1st Innings 466? Have these terminal metal numbers hung there clanking gently in the breeze ever since that dreadful night twelve years ago? Beyond and above it all across the little valley looms a relative of Table Mountain: the flat-topped, wooded mountain of Maduma, once rich with the legends of the Manica tribe, a granite altar for their tribal gods, a place of ancient sacrifice.

We take the car down the stony, pot-holed school drive, past a solitary girl lugubriously trying to fell a vast roadside tree with an axe, which is apparently the punishment for girls who misbehave. Later we are told that she is being punished for staying out late with a boyfriend, and that her penance is expected to take her three or four days of solid felling. The usual old Eagle punishment of six of the best on the bum sounds preferable and more civilised. And why should the tree, which looks perfectly healthy, be condemned to death for somebody else's fornication? The girl leans on her axe and grins at us: perhaps she thinks it was worth it.

We drive past the main sports field with its grass immaculately trimmed, and the site of the sandpit where at the start of my first term, at the age of six, I sobbed alone for hours, bereft at leaving my mother for the first time. The poignant perfume of pines reminds me of illicit cigarettes in the childish afternoon and forgotten friends like tiny 'Tammy' Thomas, and 'Bird' Wallace, and Rhodes Garwen (the only person I ever knew who was named after Cecil Rhodes) and the formidable

36

matron 'Coppers', and teachers like 'Polly' Brodsky, the spitting Hungarian who taught me French.

Suddenly there it all is before me, almost unchanged in thirty years: the low, white, red-roofed school buildings; the hall, the offices, the dormitories, the classrooms; and proudly in front, at attention, the twin flagpoles where as School Captain I would raise and lower each morning and evening the Union Jack and the school flag with the blue-and-gold Eagle badge and motto, *Arduus ad Solem*, By Strife up to the Sun. Today one flagpole is naked. The other flutters with the flag of Zimbabwe and its star and stripes of red, gold, green.

I park the car and get out. I gaze at my past, and walk in a dream.

The black groundsman, Mr Paul, who hid in terror in a cupboard on the night the murderers rampaged through the school, is a beaming little man of about fifty-five, as spruce as his gardens, with spaniel eyes and an eager moustache. He tells me that when I was at the school he supervised the swimming pool and I say I remember. He says he remembers me too. We are both lying, of course, but his lie is less ignoble than mine. Why should he remember just one out of all the hundreds of small boys he has witnessed here in nearly half a century? But I have forgotten him because in the bad old days of my childhood you simply didn't *notice* Africans much. You knew the ones at home, and they were friends, but at school they were simply there to tend the grounds and cook your food and do your laundry and you rarely asked their names.

Nearby is the office where our school secretary Audrey Belbin used to crouch warily on guard behind her old manual Remington typewriter like James Bond's faithful Miss Moneypenny, and where at the shocking age of nine we would sneak in to steal from her shelves the Star cigarettes she sold to the Africans at just one penny for eight, the sweepings of the tobacco auction floors, one old brown Rhodesian copper penny with a hole in the middle to allow the coins to be strung together like beads, and the pounds would look after themselves. The present Miss Moneypenny is a tubby, beaming black girl who taps at a smart new electric typewriter beneath the ubiquitous colour photograph of Robert Mugabe and begs to be photographed herself. Film is rare and expensive here and most Zimbabweans who spot you with a camera will beg for a portrait. Africans once were deeply suspicious of the camera, suspecting that it captured their souls, but now the security guard Miss Makarahwa too must have her picture taken and we have to promise to send copies. If this is really a school for spies then I would have to believe that Ian Fleming's Miss Moneypenny went on to become 'M', the Director-General of the British Secret Service.

The Principal of Eagle today, Miss Moyo, welcomes us into her office with tea and tomato sandwiches as dainty as any English vicar's wife could wish. She is a large lady in a nice red, black and mauve dress and smiles a great deal, broadly, and giggles a lot about her need to diet – 'I don't know why I'm so fat!' She is surely somebody's favourite aunt. Here in the Head's study too there is the usual photograph of Comrade Mugabe, and above Miss Moyo's blue steel filing-cabinet (suspiciously marked K4) there hangs a grim poster of Lenin with the slogan WORKERS OF THE WORLD UNITE. But there are also floral suburban curtains at the windows, and pelmets above, and Miss Moyo makes small talk, polite English chit-chat, introducing the school's administrative manager and giggling: 'I hate her. She keeps trying to cut my budget.' Miss Moyo shakes and quivers when she giggles, and mentions the lack of transport and the need for a school minibus to give the girls outings. Except for Lenin's disapproving scowl we could be in a primary school headmistress's office almost anywhere in England. The Head Girl, Glandeur Sibotshiwe, arrives to show us around the school and is delighted to learn that thirty-four years ago I was Head Boy here and Laurie photographs us with our arms around each other, strangers in the light, exchanging glances. She is a charming twenty-two-year-old Zulu with a jaunty scarlet ribbon in her braided hair, very friendly,

laughter and chat but also carrying a fine African dignity and a sort of grandeur. Is that why her parents called her
Glandeur? Could she be a mispronunciation, a misprint?
Laurie is quickly besotted and keeps taking pictures of her,
dozens of them. He can't leave her alone, and she loves it,
flashing her eyes and flirting with his lenses like a dark starlet.

But when I try to take my own first photograph the camera
jams immediately, mysteriously. Do the ghosts disapprove? Or
the tribal gods of Maduma? Laurie and I both wrestle with the
camera and eventually he manages to fix it. Later, on the top
games field and the site of the massacre, the girls during their
mid-morning break play stool-ball, which is very like rounders,
just as once we too played rounders there, and cricket. So little
changes. Even a brutal atrocity has left this spot a place of
recreation and the horror is forgotten. There should be something sinister about the cricket pavilion that witnessed all that
terror just yards away that night, yet it's small and banal. In the
bright morning sun there is only a feeling of sadness and
waste, and there are no spectres nor ghostly echoes of missionaries singing hymns, as they say you can still hear at night. The
only blood-red colour now against the deep green grass is the
scarlet ribbon in Glandeur's braided hair. There are snakes in
the long grass, she says, 'but I'm not afraid of snakes at all. I
only hate lizards and toads.' I ask her about the local tribal
legends connected with the mountain of Maduma. She glances
up at it dismissively and tosses her sprauncy braids. 'Is that
what it's called?' she says. 'Maduma? I didn't know.' I am astonished. How can she not know the name of this huge, brooding
African mountain that daily overshadows her African life? How
can I know about it, a white colonial exile, and she doesn't?
And what about the tribal Manica legends? 'I'm a Zulu,' she
shrugs. The proud, warlike Zulus always did treat more peaceful tribes like the Manica and the Shona with even more
contempt than the whites treated the blacks. Racism has never
been simply a matter of colour.

The girls play stool-ball with vigour in their white blouses
and light blue skirts, giggling and calling like the daughters of

Surrey stockbrokers. One of them is a vast female renowned for her football prowess, a Paul Gascoigne in a frock, and Glandeur announces that when the girl was recently sentenced to chop down a huge tree on Top Lawn – a tree that was once our rounders second base – she terrified everyone by felling it in a record forty-five minutes. 'If she was flat in front you'd think she was a man,' giggles Glandeur.

She shows us around the school, inside and out, every corner and corridor. Some things, of course, have changed. The old library has disappeared, and the gloomy boot room with its lingering odour of feet and linseed oil and urine, and the grim little lavatory cubicles, six abreast, narrow and cold and doorless to discourage masturbation. In the central quad the 'new' library, built by the Beit Trust in 1956, is no longer a library. No books. A sexy black woman teacher with braided hair begs me to send them some books. Whatever happened to all those novels by Arthur Ransome and G. A. Henty and P. C. Wren – and even Enid Blyton – that seduced our endless sultry afternoons so long ago as we lay on our narrow blue iron beds after lunch each day and dreamed our childish dreams? Claude Mellor's headmaster's study, once the centre of the universe, no longer exists: C. de C. Mellor, he signed himself, Claude de Clegg Mellor, a name that even Evelyn Waugh would never have dared to bestow on a fictional headmaster teaching in the depths of the African bush. Claude was an Oxford man in his forties, a veteran of the Dragon School, of Dunkirk, of four years in a German prisoner-of-war camp – poet, classicist, and enthusiastic director of the school's annual Shakespeare plays, one of which (*Twelfth Night*, in which I played Malvolio) we even performed in the professional Courtauld Theatre down in Umtali in front of audiences of bored teenage cuties from Marymount Convent and the Umtali Girls High School, most of them chewing gum. Claude was my boyhood idol, the teacher every writer needs, a man of great kindness and culture, of duty and decency, a man who loved writing and Latin and cricket and the great wide sweep of English history and who taught me to love them too. The rooms where he entertained the twelve-year-olds on Sunday nights with scrambled eggs and Mozart records, or Flanders and Swann, or readings from Dickens, or Edgar Allan Poe, are gone. So too is his study, once rich with the smell of security and civilisation, the cool touch of fat leather armchairs, the musty tang of books and blotting paper. In its place is only a hollow corridor leading nowhere.

Nor is it any longer possible to go splashing in the river in the valley below, at The Slide, which was once a natural helter-skelter of smooth rock over which the river flowed, a long cold watery swoop angled at thirty degrees where we often slid naked and shrieking with helpless laughter into a deep, icy pond. Today The Slide has been flooded and lies as lost as Atlantis deep in a man-made lake. By contrast what was once the 'new' swimming pool, below Bottom Field, is now almost empty. Its 'Magi-Filter' is now neither magic nor filtering because there are no spare parts. The shortage of foreign exchange, of course. A dead rat floats on the surface of the shallow, brackish water.

'Ugh!' says the Head Girl, wrinkling her nose like any English schoolgirl in a novel by Angela Brazil.

The rat is unpleasantly bloated in the sun.

'It'll explode soon,' says Laurie mischievously.

'Ugh!' shudders the Head Girl, doubtless deeply embarrassing her less fastidious Zulu ancestors, who joined unflinching battle so often with lions, elephant, and Afrikaners.

Beside the swimming pool today the little asbestos-roofed changing hut is now a Seventh Day Adventist Church with a slogan saying 'SMILE GOD LOVES YOU.' Africa today is said to be the most Christian continent of all, with churches of every possible denomination and eccentricity. The old-time white missionaries obviously did their work well and no longer inspire those cartoons where they sit simmering in cannibal cooking pots. Today there are even three black Nigerian nuns in Manchester trying to re-convert the white natives to Christanity. A sign by the door of the Eagle School Seventh Day Adventists' swimming pool changing-hut church says 'THE

EAGLE S.D.A. WELCOMES YOU ALL, FEEL FREE AND FEEL AT HOME', but the door is locked.

Otherwise very little is really different. The ghosts of the murdered missionaries may not haunt the school but the spirit of Claude Mellor's work certainly does. When we enter a classroom all the twenty-year-old girls stand up politely – just as we were taught to greet visitors so long ago. If they wore little navy blue caps outdoors, as we did, I am sure they would doff them. The concrete bases of our old cricket practice nets still lurk on the edge of the sports field in front of the school. The Sick Room, where the suffering and the slackers used to lie in a pungent haze of wintergreen and disinfectant, is still a sanatorium. On the Bottom Field, where I played soccer for the 1st XI, the trees seem huge after forty years' growth, and the cricket pitch is devastated, just bare patches of rutted earth. But the girls still play football here as well as netball.

The dining room is just as it was, though now there is a sign over the door that reads DINNING ROOM. In the hall erratic red letters above the stage say WELC ME, and the chairs are marked mysteriously K1529, K1543, and yet another portrait of Mugabe hangs beside new African honours boards, looking down on the ping-pong tables. The old tuckshop where once we queued impatiently to spend our pocket money of a shilling a week on twelve liquorice sticks, or three packets of sherbert, or a couple of fat Mars Bars, is now a secretarial office, and the classrooms boast green-and-white typewriters (K2038, K2002) and smart venetian blinds, and are no longer called Form Va or Form IVb but 'Typing and Office Practice.' But 'Practice' is spelled correctly, which it probably wouldn't be in Britain, and although one classroom has a large chart about tribalism and African clans – ZIMBABWE HISTORICAL AND ECONOMIC SYSTEMS FROM THE TIME OF SETTLER (COLONIAL) RULE – and a newspaper headline reading ROAD TO SOCIALISM TOUGH AND BRUISY, I can almost smell again in these rooms the chalk and ink of thirty-five years ago, and hear the rubber catapult squish of a wet paper pellet bouncing off the shaven short-back-and-sides bonce of one of the Gilbert twins during a Latin lesson while the master's back was turned towards the blackboard. In my fond imagination 'Polly' Brodsky from Budapest is still hurling the painfully hard blackboard eraser in the direction of some boy larking at the back of the class, and Andrew Moncreiff's ten-year-old lips are still tinged with blue from his extraordinary habit of drinking Quink, and there's still an unmistakable whiff of the pencil shavings we used to wrap in blotting paper and smoke through a Platignum pen-top during evening prep when the master on duty was playing truant and sipping a surreptitious gin and tonic. The central quad, where the guerrillas harangued the terrified pupils on that dreadful night twelve years ago, is still colourful in the sun with a blaze of flowers – pink, red, mauve. The showers still work in the rotting discoloured changing rooms that once stank of rugby boots and sweat, and the old Matron's clothes room is still a storeroom with shelves tidily stacked with skirts and T-shirts, and it is still ruled strictly by a neat matron in starched white overalls. She fusses about her looks when I ask if I can take a photograph and then begs me to send her a copy.

The dormitories that once were named (like the school itself) after birds of prey – Shrike, Augur, Falcon, Kite – are now called hostels, with names like Chimoio and Kaguni. Martial dormitory is now a sad, echoing shell of bare stained mattresses, and in most of the dormitories the paint is peeling badly and the walls are discoloured. But everywhere the blue iron beds are the very same that we slept on forty years ago, and for me Kaguni Hostel is still Falcon dormitory, where Frank Cary came and sat on my bed at night. That bed, there. That very bed? Perhaps. Glandeur and I sit on it to be photographed, but I'm damned if I'll tell her why. She would probably giggle.

It's a glorious sunny day and yet in almost every dormitory there is a girl lying 'sick' in one of the beds. Glandeur simply ignores them, but I wonder. We were never particularly ill here except for the occasional unpredictable jaundice epidemic or polio scare. So why should these girls be ill? The poor diet? Or just malingering?

The school bell – the very same handbell that I used to ring along these corridors in 1956 – summons us to eat in the 'Dinning Room', where a hundred girls settle in chairs (all individually numbered, K134, K135) on either side of long refectory tables (surely the very same tables, too) and a friendly few rush to sit next to us. They tell me their names. Angela, Florence. Angela? *Florence*? This is *Zimbabwe*, for God's sake, and we are eating African sadza and beans. And yet it could almost be the Eagle dining hall of forty years ago. Manfully Laurie and I clear our plates, grinning unconvincingly, but the girls leave most of theirs, wrinkling their noses just as we wrinkled ours at the cold cabbage and gristle of yesteryear. In the big kitchens very little has changed. I photograph the cooks and washers-up and they all demand to be sent copies.

After lunch we make a final nostalgic pilgrimage down the hill into the little valley beneath Second Forest to explore the old open-air stage where we performed the annual Shakespeare play beside the trickling mountain stream and the old swimming pool. Walls of bracken provided the wings, and *Greensleeves* the music, always *Greensleeves*, 'Greensleeves is my heart's delight, Greensleeves is my only joy', and we believed that Henry VIII had composed that haunting tune, and Prospero once tramped through this African bush like a tribal chieftain, and Macbeth once called across this equatorial valley, and Shylock, Oberon, Mark Antony. Miss Moyo and Glandeur know nothing about this secret place and are startled to learn of this old forgotten temple to the Bard in the bush, but Mr Paul the groundsman remembers and volunteers to act as guide. The grass and nettles are waist-high, the thorns tugging at our shirts and scratching our arms as we forage nervously down the hillside armed with sticks, alert for snakes, with Mr Paul ahead of us slashing a path with a scythe. Deep in the undergrowth we find the buried steps, unused for decades, archaeological evidence of a lost empire, and then eventually at the bottom of the hill not an airy open-air theatre but instead a tiny overgrown wooded glade with a stagnant pond. The open-air stage on which as a boy of ten I wore a sheet trimmed with purple, and stabbed Caesar, has been reclaimed by the jungle. The auditorium where my mother sat in a funny hat with all the other mothers in funny hats, and dreamed that her son might one day become an Olivier, has been swamped by vast weeds. The pool where I learned to swim, a skinny seven-year-old suspended in a canvas belt on the end of a pole wielded by Polly Brodsky from Budapest, is now submerged under monster ferns. The silence and sinister rustic stillness are such that it could indeed be now a scene from *The Tempest*, Illyria, *A Midsummer Night's Dream*, but in truth it seems more like Pompeii or Carthage, or a line from Ozymandias, King of Kings: 'Look on my works, ye mighty, and despair.' This silence is what it is like to be overtaken by history, to become not even a footnote.

Something grunts in the undergrowth, *hoo-hoo*, deep and gruff. 'What's that?' says the Zulu Head Girl, nervously.

Caliban, perhaps, or Bottom, or Hamlet's father's ghost.

We take some quick photographs and leave, panting back up the hill, sweating heavily.

'Why don't we open the stage again?' says the Head Girl bravely, once we have safely reached the main school driveway at the top of the hill.

Mr Paul nods without enthusiasm. Mr Paul suspects quite rightly that he is the one who would have to do all the work.

'The Head Girl is lovely, and so is Mr Paul,' I write in my diary later that night. It seems absurd to write something like that after knowing them for just a few hours, but it also seems true.

They see us back to the car and we drive away at last, waving until we are out of sight, up the track through First Forest, back towards civilisation and 1990, a dream of thirty years accomplished at last but over already, history already, the stuff of memory.

Beside Top Gate, where the school track joins the main road, where we saw the Queen Mother, we find at last the memorial to the victims of the massacre. It is outside the school grounds and not easy to find. Certainly no casual passer-by would know to what it refers. It is just a small plaque planted in the blood-red earth on the edge of a little bluff high above the school, overlooking the valley and the mountain of Maduma beyond. It reads: 'In your distress say to God, MY FATHER, I DO NOT UNDERSTAND YOU, BUT I TRUST YOU. Then you will experience His help.'

I gaze for the last time down into the valley at the scattered school buildings shimmering so white and small in the distant sunlight, and find that my eyes are brimming with ridiculous tears, and know that I shall never return, not even after another thirty years. There is no longer any need. I have seen it now. The ghosts are laid.

Away to the left, in the distance, the deep remembered range of prehistoric mountains, the granite hulks of Castle Beacon and The Saddle and Camel's Hump, stand guard high over the valley like medieval fortresses, staunch and dignified against the sky.

A thin breeze whispers in the grass.

'What a beautiful place,' says Laurie softly. 'I understand at last.'

CHAPTER 4

THE MISSIONARY POSITION: SIR GARFIELD TODD

COLONIAL RHODESIA enjoyed some pretty bizarre leaders, but the most unlikely of all was Garfield Todd, the missionary who arrived from New Zealand in 1934 when he was twenty-six, toiled for nineteen years on an African reserve hundreds of miles out in the bush, became Prime Minister for five years from 1953 to 1958, but was eventually placed under detention by Ian Smith because of his pro-black sympathies, imprisoned without trial, and nearly hanged for treason.

During the Smith regime, especially in the 1970s, Todd and his equally unfashionably liberal daughter Judith were loathed and reviled by most white Rhodesians, who sneered that they were 'kaffir-lovers', 'munt-lovers', traitors. It is startling now to remember how deeply they were hated, with a bottomless colonial malice. They were spurned in the street and scandalous stories about their private lives were put about to stain their reputations. Judy Todd escaped this poisonous atmosphere by going to London, where she lived in exile for eight years, but her father lived on bravely throughout the war of black independence in detention at the family's remote Hokonui ranch near Zvishavane and not far, appropriately, from the Great Zimbabwe ruin which is now a national symbol of black Zimbabwean pride and freedom. But if the more extreme of the right-wing white Rhodesians had known then, during those dangerous years of civil war, that Todd was indeed secretly helping Robert Mugabe's black guerrillas –

and secretly passing on information to the British Government via MI6 – they would undoubtedly have driven out to Hokonui and lynched him.

Todd was a friend of Mugabe's and had in fact given him his first job as a teacher, when Mugabe was nineteen (though neither Sir Garfield nor Lady Todd remembers what Mugabe was like then) so things changed dramatically when Mugabe came to power in 1980. Todd was immediately appointed a Senator, and he was knighted in 1985.

Today Sir Garfield Todd is a white-haired but fit, spry eight-two-year-old. 'I have a very strong constitution and I haven't wrecked it,' he says jovially. 'I've missed all the fun of riotous living.' He has an oddly squishy, cosy, grinning face and a strange accent that is part-Rhodesian, part-Antipodean, so that he pronounces 'charge' as *chaaaaj* and 'Mugabe' as *Mgaaaabe*. He and his wife Grace are obviously reasonably wealthy even though, amazingly, he has never received a Parliamentary pension despite serving twelve years in the Southern Rhodesian House (five of them as Prime Minister) and five more years in the Zimbabwean Senate. 'Not that that worries me,' he says. 'I manage to live fine, but I certainly wasn't in it for the money!' They have a second home in Bulawayo but still live in the wilds, 300 miles from Harare, in secluded luxury – complete with black girl servants, two cars, a video recorder, and a regular subscription to *The Spectator*. Their home is protected from intruders by the longest, roughest, stoniest, most rutted bushveld 'driveway' I have ever had the misfortune to tackle by car. He retired from the Senate in 1985 ('at that time I thought I was dying: no one could find out what was wrong with me; it was malaria from forty years ago') but he still writes articles for Zimbabwean newspapers and African magazines, and Lady Todd still oversees the 800 cattle on the ranch. Their days of ostracism by fellow whites are over. The bitter antagonism has evaporated. Europeans who cut him dead in the Seventies now approach in the street for a chat. 'Now I'm friends with every-body,' he grins, and Lady Todd adds: 'It's remarkable, people coming up and saying, *oh, how nice to see you.*'

He still goes down to the church in the valley for communion every Sunday, and sometimes speaks from the pulpit. 'I'm chairman of the trust that owns the whole place,' he says. 'We've been tremendously privileged. From 1934 we've been members of an African congregation. The people are enthusiastic and the singing is glorious and when you go to church on Sunday morning there's not twenty people, there's 800 people and the church is full of harmony. It's beautiful. So we have many blessings.'

On the other side of the valley they have given 3000 acres of their ranch to found a farming co-op of wounded and maimed ex-terrorists – near the site of the second Battle of Bannockburn, the Bannockburn railway station that was regularly mortared at night by the black guerrillas during the war. As we sit and sip beer (before a lunch of mince and noodles) on the Todds' airy hillside verandah, perched high above the beautiful valley, he seems a little lonely, very eager to talk and almost pathetically pleased to have new company, urging my photographer Laurie Sparham and me to stay long into the afternoon. Todd and his wife are both remarkably kind, chatty and open – even when I ask him how he, a Christian, a missionary, could possibly justify helping terrorists who were then going out from his house to kill people.

My nice, sensitive, English liberal photographer is appalled by this question and later berates me for it. 'How *could* you?' he says in dismay. 'How *could* you ask that good, distinguished old man a crass question like that?' But in fact it seems highly relevant, especially since Todd himself has just been criticising the black African 'Uncle Tom' politician Bishop Muzorewa for collaborating with the whites and Ian Smith even to the extent of becoming Minister for War. 'Muzorewa must be like an albatross around the Church's neck, the Methodist Episcopal Church,' says Todd. 'He's given up politics but he's never apologised for anything he did. As a Christian he might have done that at the beginning. Minister of War, no: that was a bad slip on the part of his Church – and himself, that he should have been Minister of War, as he was, and saying "*it made my day*" when there was a massacre somewhere. That was a very famous statement.'

So why is it acceptable for a Christian like Todd to give succour to terrorists, almost to boast of it, but not acceptable for a Christian like Muzorewa to oppose them? Just what *is* the missionary position when it comes to war, bloodshed, and murder? How was Todd able to reconcile his religious and political beliefs?

'It wasn't so difficult, you know,' he says. 'We've been here since 1934, that's fifty-six years, and we'd watched the patience of the people, and we'd seen the suffering of the people. We saw the attempts they made, always ready to negotiate, as they've always been. We'd seen the violence of Smith, the violence of the people, the violence of the soldiers. We'd seen people that we know and love killed and hurt, and there comes a point when ... it's not a case of patience running out, it's a case of feeling this is the only way that you're going to stop this horror. It's defensive. So I really didn't have any problem with that. I didn't refuse to be called up in the war. I wasn't shipping arms. We gave food.

'In the late Seventies everything was horrible. From round here you could on occasions see a gunship spraying bullets out over on the villages near that mountain – and the Boys, of course, lived in the mountain.'

'You say *the Boys*. You mean the guerrillas.'

'Yes. The Guerrillas. The Boys.'

'You were helping them actively?'

'Yes.'

'Not with weapons?'

'No, no, no. No, no, no. Just their toothpaste and stamps and food and boots and things like that. Sometimes Mugabe's lot, ZANLA, left their guns and their pistols and their rockets here. They were told to keep away from this house, but we kept our school open throughout the war. We had very good relations with the guerrillas.'

'Didn't you have revenge attacks on you by Smith's forces? They must have known what was going on here.'

'They did. My best friend twenty miles along the road was killed, a miner here was killed, a lot of whites were killed, and we came through utterly safely, of course. There's a book called *Meet Me in November* – that was the phrase they used when they sought permission to kill somebody: if the reply was *"meet me in November"* that was permission to go ahead and kill, and according to this book two or three Selous Scouts came down to this area to kill a black Lutheran doctor at the mission near here, and me. In the middle of the night they knocked on his door and he got out of bed and went to the door and there were two shots and that was the doctor. They didn't get me, though there were other stories that they tried.'

'Were you afraid?'

'Well, I suppose we were.'

'We were in the night,' says Lady Todd, 'when the dog barked and you didn't know.'

'You came out here in your dressing gown,' says Sir Garfield, 'and could see fifteen or twenty armed men running up to here, and for a moment you don't know who they are or what they're going to do. And then you find they're ZANLA chaps all over the place and want food. That's fine. But you don't know what's going to happen.'

Lady Todd chips in again: 'There was a thing that was really amusing but wasn't amusing, of course. One night some young guerrillas came and had actually been given a command not to come here, not to endanger the situation by coming, but this group had just come in from Mozambique, quite young chaps, and they came to get food and we didn't have all that much . . .'

Sir Garfield takes up the story: 'I walked out about a mile and chose a place where I'd put food the next day. There was a big group of security forces camped here at the side of the mountain, and another guard over here by the waterworks, and they would occasionally put ambushes on the road. This night I went out with these chaps and we chose the places and came back. Next day I took some bread and Cokes and put them in the right place.'

Lady Todd: 'This had all been done so secretly, but the next night there they are under the orange trees. They'd come to say goodbye, and thank me – and they'd brought back the empty Coke bottles!'

Eventually, of course, this clandestine activity – which was understandably nothing less than treason in the eyes of other whites – caught up with Todd and he was arrested on a capital charge of assisting the guerrillas. Luckily for him this didn't happen until 1980, by which time the war was over, the British had taken over the Government with Lord Soames as the interim Governor before black independence, and Ian Smith was no longer in charge. Had Smith still been in control, or had Bishop Muzorewa won the post-independence election as the British expected, Todd might well have been hanged. As it was he was at first refused bail: 'not on a capital charge,' said the magistrate ominously.

'I was taken to the prison in Shabane [*now Zvishavane*],' says Todd, 'no whites there, everybody was black, and I had to take off all my clothes except my underpants. They took my watch, and then they gave me prison garments but they were all too small. They got me some trousers (with no buttons) that were far too big. But Judith got in touch with a man from *The Times* who got in touch with Soames, and the magistrate was called back from golf, reopened the court, and said I'd be remanded again out of custody. It was just as close as anything to Muzorewa taking over. I would have been sunk. Smith and Muzorewa would have gone ahead.'

Todd's affection for the African people of Zimbabwe ('*kaffir-lover!*') goes back fifty-six years, ever since he and his wife first came to Rhodesia. I tell him that I am astonished by the racial harmony of modern Zimbabwe and by the magnanimity of blacks towards whites after all the bitterness and bloodshed of the civil war.

He shrugs. 'You see, this is something I knew,' he says. 'That's the reason I went into politics in the first place. We came here in 1934 and we were living in the African area, in what was known as the Lundi Reserve at that time. When we

arrived there had been other whites but because of the
Depression and so on they'd all moved, and our Board in New
Zealand were horrified to think of a young man and his wife
– I was twenty-six, Grace was twenty-three – living amongst
20,000 blacks with no other whites in the area. So they wrote
and said they were so sorry things had worked out this way
and by the end of the year they'd have at least one more couple
out here to give us someone to talk to. It was thirteen years
before the next couple arrived, and that was our salvation,
because everything had to be done with the people – all the
schools, churches, had to be developed, not by two people
but together.

'When I went into politics my wife and I decided that maybe
I could get across to the electorate, which was white, the fact
that the real potential of this country was not minerals and
agriculture but *people*, whom we had come to know and love
and serve, and who were unknown to the mass of white
people. They just didn't know them, and that's why it was
impossible for them to consider negotiating for the extension
of political power over an area which would have given us a
base of security in this country, of black and white – the very
thing that de Klerk is trying to do in South Africa. How he's
going to do it, I don't know, but he's got things working for
him that I didn't have. He's got a world understanding, he's
got a world atmosphere of negotiation, he's got that very strong
business community whose whole future is absolutely in jeop-
ardy at the present time, so these things could make it that de
Klerk *will* win. He's *got* to win. But really, honestly, when I
think of what I went through . . .'

There is a sudden wet snorting from the valley below.

'Do you hear that?' says Lady Todd quietly. 'Hippo. Hippo
down in the river.'

'The blacks would have talked to me,' says Todd with pas-
sion, and there is an echoing sadness about his voice, a hollow
memory of lost chances so foolishly squandered. 'They still
would have listened. They wouldn't listen to Whitehead
[*Todd's successor as Prime Minister*] but they would have

listened to me. I could have done it if I'd had the support of the whites. In the 1950s, when the whites were ready to dispense with me, I said to them: "this is your last chance. If you throw me out then there's no thought in the mind of the African that any white Government is going to give them the terms that they want." And my last indiscretion was to set up a commission on the franchise. I wasn't suggesting to the whites (because it would've been crazy) that we'd have universal franchise at that time, but that teachers, policemen, doctors, nurses – all the people who were leaving the Tribal Trust areas and coming in to the white economy – should be voters. De Klerk is having the same problem now except that he's got a lot more in his favour. De Klerk was asked the other day whether there was anything to be learned from Zimbabwe's experience and he said, "yes, they didn't start negotiating soon enough." Now, I was called a man ahead of my time: so what was the time? Twenty years before me.

'I wasn't ahead of my time. Rab Butler, who was the great man on the Indian side, with all his experience there, said that when a Government such as mine, racial and minority, decided that it was time to make changes and give concessions, it was already too late. All right, then it's too late in South Africa. I don't believe it, you know, but they're going to have some tough times.'

His face creases with pain as he remembers the difficulties and battles of those years as Prime Minister. 'Big business, none of them were on my side, I never got anything,' he says sadly. Apart from his wife his only fan then seems to have been his daughter Judy, who felt he was capable of anything, even of saving the Hungarians when they were invaded by the Russians in 1956. Judy then was thirteen and could not accept that her father was powerless to defend Hungary: he was Prime Minister, wasn't he? Well, then.

Todd has no time at all for Ian Smith – when I told him I was going to see Smith in Harare he said dismissively 'give him five minutes' – but he does agree with Smith on one thing: the endless perfidy of British Governments in their dealings with Rhodesia. Every white Rhodesian politician, from liberal Todd to middle-of-the-road Welensky to right-wing Smith, is disgusted (I suspect quite rightly) by the way British politicians betrayed their trust in Central Africa. The Rhodesians, without exception, expected the British to play cricket, but the British kept changing the rules. The Rhodesians still believed in British imperial standards of excellence that the British themselves had cynically abandoned. The British red that had once coloured a quarter of the world atlas was now no more than a blush on the face of devious British politicians.

'I didn't have a hope as Prime Minister because Britain wouldn't help me,' says Todd sadly. 'She didn't see that there was any necessity, any threat to the future. In 1953 I wanted five million pounds to start doing African housing so that people could own their own housing outside the cities, but I was given only a million eventually. Even during the war, when I was working with MI6 here – and no doubt MI6 were handing on my views and information to the British Government – there was no sense of urgency, no understanding. They didn't even think Mugabe would win until about a week before the election.

'I've got to do an article for *Drum* magazine and the subject is: could the war have been avoided? Well, if you're going at 100 miles an hour, and another chap is coming at 100 miles an hour the other way, and you meet on the corner, that's an accident, and it's unavoidable. But there in 1954 and 1955 I was saying, "this is what we've got to do to stop a collision." Of course it's avoidable. If it wasn't avoidable then it's not avoidable in South Africa.

'If I'd got my way, more and more Africans would have come on to the voters' roll. The whites at the moment are the key thing in South Africa, and they were the key here. If we'd had a few more blacks on the roll I could have got away with it. De Klerk *hasn't* got blacks on the roll and he's now got to convert the whites, which is a *very* difficult job.'

Despite his criticisms of the British, Sir Garfield acknowledges that the Lancaster House agreement, which finally transferred power from whites to blacks in 1980, was 'very good' for Zimbabwe.

But he is splendidly contemptuous of Ian Smith, the man he believes might once have come so close to having him hanged for treason.

'I still meet him at the occasional cattle sale,' says Todd, 'but we don't have any conversation. The last time I talked to him was after I was out of detention and I went to him to try to persuade him to take a different line, telling him that he still would have the whites behind him and only he could change their situation. He just smiled his frosty smile.'

'Would he have seen the error of his ways by now, or not?'

'No! No! This would have been a *wonderful* country if he'd been allowed to carry on.'

'It's a wonderful country now.'

'No, no, no, no, it's full of problems. You ask him. He'll detail them. He's probably got them printed and will give them to you on a slip.'

'Is it true that a lot of Africans are quite fond of Ian Smith?'

'That's what he says.'

By contrast Todd is a great admirer of his old friend (and employee) Robert Mugabe, even though he is openly critical of many of Mugabe's policies, especially his dream of a one-party Marxist state.

'I think you must give him most marks for bringing the two groups together, ZANU and ZAPU, the Ndebele and Shona,' says Todd. 'Mugabe's a great man, and not just because of reconcili- ation. A lot of people get a reasonable university degree if they have the opportunity, but with no opportunity, and everything against him, he eventually got *five*. By the beginning of the 1960s no Africans really thought that they could run the coun- try. They were looking for better conditions, and changing this, and alleviating that, and so on. It was not for them to become the Government, and one of his jobs was to convert them to the idea that they *could* run the country. So then he had a *terrible* time, you know. One day a security bod who used to come and visit me when I was in detention, to keep an eye on me (we were sitting here having tea one morning) said that the worst job he'd ever had to do was to go to Mugabe and tell him that his little boy was ill, and then to go back and tell him that the little boy had died, and then go back and tell him, no, he would not be allowed to go to the funeral. These are *inhumane* things, aren't they? Smith, anybody, me I hope – anyone who's in charge of the Government – would surely have made arrangements.'

'Why wouldn't Smith allow him to go to the funeral?'

'Just the usual thing of white and black. These were horrible things. The whole time, especially in the late Seventies, everything was horrible.'

Mugabe was raised by the Jesuits and Todd believes that he is still a Christian, 'though he was really vitriolic about the Church on television the night before last. He said that because he wouldn't obey them they refused to give his mother communion. I think it was a horrible thing to do.'

Can Mugabe the ex-terrorist, the Marxist, *really* be a Christian?

'Well,' says Todd, 'give us the definition of a Christian.'

'You know better than I do.'

He laughs: 'Right, I ought to, that's what I was trained in. I would say that, yes, the influence of the Church on his life has been tremendous and still is.'

He makes Mugabe sound almost angelic, but even so Sir Garfield reckons that it will soon be time for Mugabe to think about retiring now that he has had more than ten years in power. 'Not even an angel should go on for more than fifteen years,' he says. 'Roosevelt got four terms and that was one too many. Mugabe's got five years – I hope no longer – to really bring us all together.'

When Todd was rushed to hospital in Bulawayo in 1989 after suffering bad petrol burns on his face and body ('it was touch and go, a grim time: it could have killed me') President Mugabe and Joshua Nkomo came to visit him, and Mugabe has told him that he is always available if Todd wants to see him. So they are friends. But Todd is still quite prepared to criticise the President, sometimes in a surprisingly flippant manner.

'It's not a democracy but it never was, was it? Zimbabwe is a socialist democracy but we haven't started on the democracy,' he jokes, laughing loudly when Lady Todd protests.

'Perhaps we should say he's started on the democracy but not on the socialism,' Todd chuckles. 'But now that Julius Nyerere has been in touch with God – Marx wasn't, that's where he made a mistake, because Marx thought the one-party state was absolutely tops – but Julius has recently been in touch with God and in this morning's *Chronicle* he says that God has not ordained the one-party state, but unfortunately he can't give us a quote that God has forbidden the one-party state.

'I don't think Mugabe's perfect and I'm afraid that the very qualities that he's got – his devotion to the people, dedication to the people, his determination to get things done, his ability – and maybe if he thinks this is the last five years (which he ought to do) then he might just determine to do what he has promised, or threatened, and that is use legislation to bring in a one-party state. And that I'm afraid of.'

'There's far more talk now amongst ordinary black people against the idea of a one-party state,' suggests Lady Todd.

'Yes, I think so,' says Sir Garfield. 'Not all of them. Some of them think that anything Mugabe says will be right, and they've got a lot to thank him for. We've all got a lot to thank him for. But things haven't worked out just as easily as he expected. You know, we didn't sign that guarantee for investors in 1980 or '81 when we should have done, but without apologies in 1989 we *do* sign it. So we've lost nine years.

'There are plenty of opponents of the one-party state in the Party.'

Todd is sharply critical of some of Mugabe's ministers: 'The Minister of Home Affairs is really a Minister of Words. He blubbers words, words, words, words, but nothing happens. He says for example that within no time the lorries and buses will be doing eighty kilometres an hour, but unless they're going uphill you never seen them doing eighty, they're always over a hundred.'

He is appalled by ministerial corruption: 'A lot of people now are getting hard currency that should never be getting it. There's a lot of corruption. Some ministers are in jail and ought to be in jail. Mugabe's been rightly concerned about the corruption of his ministers. This was a *horrible* thing, and then there was great criticism of Mugabe for stepping in for [*Frederick*] Shava when Shava should have gone to jail for perjury. And then Shava is now put back in a position in the party, so people have been voting for corruption, which is very, very serious. One wonders if some of the people think that honesty and integrity are white qualities.'

'Now that's a very cynical remark, if I may say so,' says Lady Todd, shocked.

'I don't often make cynical remarks,' says Todd, 'but that's a cynical remark. I'm only saying I don't know how they vote for Shava, and one wonders *why* they vote for Shava. He had to pay an enormous fine, anyway.'

Both Sir Garfield and Lady Todd suggest that part of the corruption problem may be that Mugabe may still owe old debts of friendship to some of his ministers that may go back many years to the days when they were all in exile together, fighting for freedom in the bush against Ian Smith's ruthless regime. 'It's very close still to all that dreadful time of the struggle,' Lady Todd points out, 'and none of us knows all the experiences Mugabe had with these chaps down in Mozambique and in other parts. We don't know how much they helped him.'

Mugabe is even well aware of the rumours about his wife Sally (*Amai*) Mugabe's alleged involvement in the Willowgate scandal, says Todd: 'When the Sandura Commission [*which investigated ministerial corruption in Zimbabwe*] handed over their second report they said they had gone into every accusation they had heard, including accusations about Amai Mugabe, and Mugabe said "*oh, you mean about sending cars up to Ghana?*"'

'And they said yes,' interjects Lady Todd, 'and they had not been able to find any proof of anything like that at all.'

Todd is particularly critical of the Zimbabwean Press, which has been so cowed and browbeaten by Mugabe (except for the pink independent *Financial Gazette*) that it fawns and cringes in a morass of self-censorship.

'It's disastrous,' says Todd, and he describes how he tried recently to have an article arguing against the one-party state published in the Harare *Sunday Mail* but the editor, 'my friend Mr Chikerema', refused to publish it, so Todd tried to persuade the paper's advertising department to publish it as a paid advertisement but was told that the editor had the right to veto it. 'Friends of mine say they can't get their letters published either in the *Sunday Mail*,' says Todd. 'Chikerema once said *China's done more for mankind than either Britain or America*, so that gives you the level of his intelligence.'

Above all, Todd is particularly perturbed about the frighteningly high level of unemployment, especially among schoolleavers, which he sees as a timebomb ticking away under Mugabe's regime. 'It's getting on for a million unemployed and there's only a million in jobs,' he says. 'Unemployment is fifty per cent of those who'd like jobs. It's terrible.

'Basically we can feed all our people, so no one should starve in this country, whether he's got a job, or is a cripple, or anything. It just needs organisation.

'The Government is so firmly in the saddle – and it's the best thing that it should be – but the future is not absolutely safe when you begin to get nearly a million young people aged eighteen on the voters' roll. If they organised themselves a little bit they could demand a whole lot more than the unemployed are getting today. Well, they're getting nothing, of course. The group of unemployed is a very large one and could sway any issue if they were organised. The students have had a rough time.'

I suggest that the opposition to Mugabe now comes no longer from whites, who are generally delighted with him for all that he has done to preserve their powerful influence and enviable standard of living, but from disgruntled blacks who believe that he hasn't delivered – that after ten years in power he hasn't given his own black supporters what he promised them when they were fighting for freedom and independence.

'I think this is actually a fair comment,' says Lady Todd. 'It's the land thing that's the big thing.'

Sir Garfield disagrees: 'Is it? I don't know that it is. It's jobs. They wouldn't worry about the land if there were plenty of jobs, but if you can't get a job then you're looking for land.'

Surprisingly, considering Todd's admiration for Mugabe and contempt for Ian Smith, he agrees with Smith rather than Mugabe (and with Mugabe's vitriolic opponent Edgar Tekere) that Zimbabwe now needs to embrace capitalism and a free economy (but 'capitalism with a human face') rather than Marxism, and to relax its present restrictive currency and investment controls, if it is to begin to solve its problems.

'Mugabe's becoming more and more pragmatic,' says Todd. 'He's beginning to realise that the money which he is spending comes from the private enterprise sector. That's what they're trying to do now by devaluing the currency. The World Bank tells us that our dollar is worth too much money on the open market. The idea is that the dollar will go down over the next two or three years until it's worth perhaps ten pennies [*instead of 25p, as at present*]. Now, at ten pennies nobody's going to buy motorcars or new machines unless it's a big company. It's a very horrible way of doing it but it's a very sensible way, and then they can take off all controls, like New Zealand did, but I don't think New Zealand devalued as much as we are thinking to do. Obviously if you can devalue by twenty per cent a year for three years then you *can* let people do what they want with the currency, because it's not overvalued and you're not going to lose much of your currency on that basis. If they do that then they're able to take their profits out.'

So what of Zimbabwe's future? Are the Todds both optimistic?

'Yes, very,' says Lady Todd.

'Very,' says Sir Garfield, 'unless there's a one-party state.'

But Mugabe has dreamed of a one-party state for so long that it's inevitable, isn't it?

'No, I don't think so,' says Todd. 'They could only do it if

61

the people are convinced that it's a good thing to do, but they mightn't be. If members of parliament don't think that people are behind a one-party state they won't support it.'

What, Mugabe's own loyal, browbeaten ZANU Party MPs would actually vote against him in parliament to prevent him setting up his one-party state? Todd seems quite genuinely to think so.

If he's right, Zimbabwe must surely be the strangest 'Marxist dictatorship' ever, and Britain's legacy in Central Africa of parliamentary democracy and the rule of law must be stronger and much less tarnished than some of us ever thought.

CHAPTER 5

THE OLD WHITE RHINO:
IAN SMITH

THE MOST remarkable example of Robert Mugabe's states-manlike policy of reconciliation between the races is the fact that Ian Smith, Rhodesia's last white Prime Minister, still lives in Zimbabwe's capital city and is still allowed openly to criticise Mugabe and his Government in the most vociferous terms.

He has called the Government 'totally evil' but still rides his bicycle around the roads of Salisbury (now Harare) and his letters are still headed 'The Hon. I. Douglas Smith, GCLM, ID' and he has started writing his memoirs.

Any other 'Marxist dictator' coming at last to power after ten years in detention and then a vicious fifteen-year civil war, as Mugabe did, would have taken a jubilant revenge on Ian Smith and would probably have had him swiftly hanged from the nearest lamp post. Indeed, Mugabe himself once said that Smith should have been hanged 'and hanged publicly.' It was Smith, after all – 'Good Old Smithy' to his white supporters – whom many Africans considered to be the arch racist and fascist who had oppressed them for so long, and they blamed him for slaughtering 30,000 of their comrades and brothers and sisters and children in his bloody defence of white supremacy. It was Smith who had said that 'never in a thousand years' would he accept black majority rule in Rhodesia. It was Smith who had declared white Rhodesia's independence from Britain in 1965 – with patriotic irony on 11 November, Remembrance Day – and had held the might of the entire world at bay for fifteen years despite United Nations sanctions against him. It was Smith who had forced the black nationalists to take up arms and to fight for their freedom by launching their war against white Rhodesia from their inhospitable bush camps across the borders of Zambia and Mozambique. It was Smith and his notoriously ruthless Selous Scouts whom they blamed for numerous atrocities during the war. And Mugabe is said to have had a very special personal reason for hating him: when Mugabe's young son died Smith refused to allow Mugabe out of detention to go to the funeral, I was told by Sir Garfield Todd.

Smith denied the story of Mugabe's son's funeral when I taxed him with it, and said: 'It's news to me. I didn't know Mugabe when he was in detention. You must remember that he wasn't the leader of the blacks when I came to power: Nkomo and Sithole were.'

Smith also denied the African guerrillas' claim that it was not they but his own Selous Scouts who had massacred the missionaries at my old prep school: 'There's absolutely no truth in it. Subsequently we captured their chaps with diaries that proved they were involved.'

It is fascinating, too, to hear Smith claiming now that his 'never in a thousand years' remark was taken out of context ('twisted') and to listen to many of his other post-mortems. He claims now, for instance, that he never had anything against Rhodesia's black politicians ('I didn't *know* any') and that when he was Prime Minister there were many blacks who were much richer than he was.

Yet one white Zimbabwean politician, who knows both Smith and Mugabe well, told me: 'Smith is a cold, remote fish eighty per cent of the time, but *can* be sentimental and caring twenty per cent of the time. He would treat even his Cabinet colleagues like dirt, making them stand in his office and wait before suddenly looking up and saying "yes?" Mugabe was much warmer, and would leave his desk and come over for a chat.'

Mugabe's opportunity to revenge himself on Smith as soon as he came to power was of course in theory (and in law) limited by the Lancaster House Agreement that ended the civil war and that both of them signed with Britain, which stipulated that there should be no recriminations. But Smith himself had been the most notorious lawbreaker of the decade, and black lawyers could well have argued that he was a war criminal who deserved his own Nuremberg Trial. So why didn't Mugabe merely arrange for him to be the victim of an unfortunate car smash, or to be murdered by 'burglars' on his remote ranch out in the bush? Why didn't Mugabe simply play Henry II and ask some of his black knights to rid him of this turbulent pest? The world, even Britain, would only have shrugged: well, he had it coming, we would have said; he did push his luck, did Smith. Instead Smith admits that at first Mugabe actually treated him cordially in private, despite his long detention and the war and all the killings. Mugabe even admitted to Smith that he had inherited from him 'the Jewel of Africa' and allowed him to sit for many more years in Parliament not only as an MP but also as Leader of the Opposition.

Smith is utterly ungrateful for this extraordinary display of Mugabe's magnanimity. He gazes at you with the show belligerence of some huge bad-tempered beast, the last of the old white rhinos – tough, brave, short-sighted, nearly extinct, and very very cross. One white ex-Minister told me in Harare an amazing story about Smith's incredible behaviour when Mugabe finally came to power in 1980:

'Smith actually demanded a place in Mugabe's Government! Mugabe told him that he was quite unacceptable to the blacks – surely he could see that? – but Smith was very grumpy about it. You won't believe this, but at one stage Mugabe and Smith were sitting on a sofa holding hands while Mugabe explained the realities of the situation!'

I still find it impossible to visualise this scene of the white supremacist Ian Smith and the black Marxist nationalist Robert Mugabe holding hands on an English sofa, but my informant swears it happened. If so, it reinforces my belief that the rules in Zimbabwe are still the rules of cricket and completely different from the rules anywhere else in Africa. Where else in Africa would a man like Smith be allowed to live in peace, and as well as he does, after such a bitter racial war? Where else in

Africa would a man like Smith be able to sue a government newspaper like the *Sunday Mail*, as he did, and win an apology and damages simply because the paper had alleged that his butcher father Jack had been known slightingly in Scotland as '14-ounce Smith'? When I telephoned Smith one night in Harare the black ex-directory supervisor put me through with no trouble at all, and although the line echoed ominously – and Smith announced airily that his telephone was tapped – he spoke quite openly and bluntly.

Now seventy-two, Ian Smith still has a farm out in the bush but a manager runs it for him and he spends most of his time in Harare, where he lives with his wife Janet in a quiet, secluded avenue in the leafy suburb of Belgravia. Just round the corner is Smith Street ('no, it's not named after me') and right next door – with splendid irony when you consider Smith's hatred of communism – is the Cuban embassy. The embassy bristles with tall aerials and electronic security devices, and huddles secretively behind high walls and locked gates, but Smith's gates stand wide open to the street and to any potential assassin. There are no guards, no dogs. You simply walk up to the front porch and ring the bell and Smith himself opens the door. 'I don't allow myself to think about the danger,' he says later.

It's eerie to hear again after so many years those brusque, clipped, narrow Rhodesian vowels that became so familiar to us in Britain twenty-five years ago, when he defied the world and filled our TV screens, and to look at such close quarters at that narrow, determined, colonial face with the eye damaged during the Second World War when he was a pilot in the RAF and fought so bravely for freedom – a battle he firmly believes he has been fighting all his life.

It's eerie, too, to be meeting him the day after Nelson Mandela has flown out of Harare after his first visit to Zimbabwe since his release from prison in South Africa. Yesterday I saw Mandela and Mugabe together at Harare airport and revelling in all the panoply of modern African power: the howling motorcade, the Mercedes Benz with the black windows, the crooked red carpet on the runway, the armed soldiers packed into trucks, their rifles defying the sky. To see Mandela and Smith on consecutive days is to witness a quarter of a century of African history in twenty-four hours. In a month's time the Lancaster House Agreement runs out: Zimbabwe's independence treaty with Britain that for ten years has protected Smith and the whites from full black majority rule and has so far deterred Mugabe from introducing the one-party Marxist state of which he dreams.

Smith's hair now is white and he has not been well – he was in hospital recently and three weeks ago there were prayers offered up for him by the black priest in Harare's Anglican cathedral – but he still looks lean and fit and weirdly young in his brown-and-white checked shirt and beige slacks. And he is still utterly unrepentant about everything. You might accuse Ian Smith of many things, but never of being uncertain of himself. In his eyes he has always fought for freedom and the British way of life, and he still is.

We sit in fat armchairs in his impossibly English living room with its chintzy furnishings and plates hanging on the wall and shelves of blue-and-white pottery, and start chatting about our mutual acquaintance Sir John Junor, the legendary *Sunday Express* editor. Smith chuckles drily (*heh-heh-heh*) when I tell him that Junor has recently left the *Sunday Express* after the appointment of a young new editor and is now writing a column for the London tabloid *Mail on Sunday*, a paper about which Junor had often been contemptuous. Junor and Smith are friends of a sort, and Junor was one of Smith's few allies in the British media when Smith declared UDI in 1965, and constantly supported Smith's efforts 'to preserve civilisation in Central Africa.' I had then just joined the *Sunday Express* as a twenty-two-year-old reporter but was soon also writing leader articles, and when in March 1968 Smith was about to hang six more blacks I wrote a leader, under the headline SHOW THEM MERCY, urging him to reprieve them and pointing out that he had already made his point that he was now the *de facto* ruler of Rhodesia and that the prerogative of supreme power was mercy. By reprieving the six men now he would be underlining his independence and making it plain to the world precisely who was now in charge in Rhodesia. 'A brilliant leader, Graham,' said Junor. 'Ian can't possibly ignore that.' Smith did ignore it and the six men were hanged the next day.

It does not seem to be quite the time to remind him of this, not just now, not in his chintzy suburban living room in 1990.

Smith is still surprisingly deeply involved in politics and has another meeting this morning. His new white party, CAZ (Conservative Alliance of Zimbabwe), is actively supporting the black anti-Mugabe party ZUM (Zimbabwe Unity Movement) in the general election in three weeks' time. ZUM is led by Edgar Tekere, once one of Mugabe's ministers but now standing against him for the Presidency. Tekere is a frightening man whose rolling eyeballs are alarmingly manic and who once appalled Zimbabwe's whites by admitting that he had led a gang of ex-guerrillas who had killed a white farmer. How on earth can Smith now support a presidential candidate like that? The reason is that Tekere has now decked himself out in the fancy dress of a Thatcherite pro-Western capitalist – and that Smith's contempt for Mugabe is now so great that he will do almost anything and support almost anyone in his dogged determination to oust him. Smith's criticisms of Mugabe and his Government, his accusations of corruption and incompetence, are so scathing that any other African leader would surely have had him imprisoned years ago. He denounces Mugabe as being small-minded, and sneers at his plan for a one-party state, and talks of intimidation and abuse of power. He claims that the general election is being rigged and even that some of Mugabe's own black ministers complain to him privately about Mugabe's 'bankrupt Marxist philosophy.' The possibility that Mugabe's own ministers secretly consort behind his back with Smith is, I suppose, no more startling than the possibility that Smith and Mugabe once sat on a sofa holding hands.

Yet despite all Smith's open contempt and criticisms – and when he speaks to me he speaks in fusillades of furious italics – Mugabe not only tolerates his outbursts but has even recently supported Smith's claim in the courts for back payment of his MP's salary after he was suspended by Parliament in 1987 for making 'treasonous' remarks. In public Mugabe and his party, ZANU-PF, are virulent in their attacks on Smith and his supporters – which is odd considering Smith has been out of parliament for three years and is considered by most whites to be a spent force and no longer their champion. One embittered white veteran of the civil war suggested to me: 'Ask Smith whether he still thinks the war and all those deaths and maimings were really worth it.' If a white can say that, why should Mugabe take Smith seriously any longer? Yet the government newspaper *The Herald* has just accused Smith of 'crawling out of the woodwork' and Mugabe's party's general election manifesto mentions Smith by name and warns ominously:

> Some of these racists and colonialists have very short memories. Although we have forgiven them, we have not forgotten how they ill-treated and exploited our people. We shall soon have to remind them of their past, and also tell them what to expect from us in the future.

It also jeers that the election pact between Smith's and Tekere's parties is a 'hotch-potch of drunkards, embezzlers and lunatics.' But is any of this serious, or is it merely rhetoric, some complicated Zimbabwean Ruritanian game? Four months after the election – in which Tekere won an astonishing twenty-five per cent of the presidential vote – Smith was freely allowed to fly to London and was sitting in Downing Street briefing Mrs Thatcher on the realities of Southern Africa.

Back in Ian Smith's cosy living room in Harare I start by asking him why he is still so actively involved in politics when all that he fought for seems to him to have been betrayed.

'When you've been through as much as I've been through you can't just step out of it very easily,' he says. 'The poor white people of our country are destabilised, they've been pushed around and subjected to pressures, to intimidation, and the

Government are paranoic about the previous "white colonial racists" and they never stop harassing people, especially if they want to divert attention from their failings, their misdoings. So I do have a lot of white people coming to see me, writing, telephoning, and my dreams of pulling out and having a quiet life, I'm afraid, have not materialised. I find in fact that I spend more time here than I do on my farm.'

I ask him how he and his right-wing white party CAZ (he is its honorary president) can possibly support Tekere and ZUM in the general election.

'Because that is the party which represents our views, our ideas,' he says, 'and I would say I think the views of the vast mass not only of white people but black people as well, but perhaps more so the white people because Tekere is saying in public what a number of Mugabe's ministers have said to me in private but *won't* say in public, mainly that it is now clear that Marxist Leninism is a failure. Tekere is saying this in public, and that therefore we must abandon that bankrupt philosophy and we must go back to the system which worked here and which in fact works everywhere in the world where it is operated – that's the free enterprise system. He has also come out strongly in his condemnation of the corruption and nepotism of this government, and he has said it's time the government of this country worked with white people instead of driving white people away and driving them *out* of the country, bring them *in* and work with them. In fact one of Mugabe's ministers said to me – I won't mention names, obviously – that if he had a wish it would be that we could get back to this country all the white people who have left because there has been, as no doubt you are aware, a very serious brains and skills drainage from this country. We've lost two-thirds of our white people and I believe this country will progress in keeping with the number of white people they can keep, especially the white people who *were* members of this country, old white Rhodesians. You *can* bring in expatriates, you *can* import professionalism, a certain amount of skills, but what you can't import are people who have experience of

Africa, who *know* Africa and know how to *work* in Africa. That's what we've lost, and you *cannot* import that through bringing in expatriates.'

I tell Smith that I am surprised that Mugabe still seems so alarmed by him and his party: 'There's an extraordinary attack on you in the ZANU manifesto which I read in the *Herald* a couple of days ago.'

'I haven't seen that.'

'They talk about the Smith colonialists and they refer to Tekere's lot as a gang of drunkards, embezzlers and lunatics.'

'That's because that's what *they* are.'

'Are they?'

Smith chuckles drily. He chuckles drily a lot. 'Course they are,' he says. 'You will find that whenever this government says they are going to do something you can rest assured they're doing the opposite. And that's typical communist tactics. This must be one of the most corrupt governments in the world, and when one sees the reports of this Sandura Commission [*which investigated ministerial corruption in Zimbabwe*] it gives you an idea but only a *small* idea, because anybody who knows anything about what is going on in this country will tell you this Sandura Commission has only exposed the tip of the iceberg. There were many other people who everybody knew were seriously implicated, high-up people, and that's why the Sandura Commission, which was supposed to have gone on to do another exercise, was suddenly stopped.'

'How high up do you think the corruption goes?'

'Well, very high.' He thinks about this slowly, and picks his words hesitantly. 'I can't mention names, but very high.' He thinks about it again, and broods.

I ask: 'You'll be voting, presumably, on March 28?'

'Sure.'

'And voting for ZUM, your ZUM candidate.'

'Quite right.'

'And for Tekere as President.'

'Quite right. He's our only hope.'

'He has a very violent past, hasn't he? A murky past.'

71

'Same as the rest of them,' says Smith caustically. 'Tell me one who hasn't. But this is what people say: "look at Tekere, he murdered that white man out here, didn't he?" But I want to know which one of these chaps *didn't* murder innocent people – women and children. When one recounts the history of what these chaps did it's a pretty horrific story.'

'People I've spoken to have suggested that the election's going to be rigged anyway.'

'Well, it's already been rigged. It will go on being rigged every day. There is a Ministry of Political Affairs here which in Mugabe's words is there specifically to promote ZANU-PF: to have offices through the country with incumbents supplied by the government, transport supplied by the government, paid for by the government, to promote ZANU-PF. Those were his words. This has been going on for some time, so clearly there's a lot of money – and it runs into millions, taxpayers' money – which has been used to promote the party. All the rallies which have been held over the last month or so through the country for the nomination of candidates, government transport has been used for those, civil servants have been used for those, policemen in *uniform* have been there helping and counting the votes. They don't hide that. Then two days before nomination day it was brought to my attention that there were no voters' rolls available, there were no maps of the Delimitation Commission which recently sat, but government members of parliament all had them, and high-up government officials. But for other people – and we have a written record of this from the officer in the registrar's office – they are not available. That was three days before nomination day. So how can you determine your constituency and get voters on the voters' roll? You've got to get them to sign your nomination form. Then this government has had for the last month an average of two hours a day prime television time supporting their party and their candidates. No opposition members had one minute. In Monday's paper the whole of the editorial page, two full pages, was a print of their manifesto. It is quite clear that already the thing has been rigged. The nomination of one of the ZUM candidates was turned down because he put in his nomination form with a cheque and they said "we don't accept cheques, you've got to produce cash". *But – BUT –* the same day or the next day Mugabe's nomination for President was handed in and there was old Zvobgo [*the Minister of State for Political Affairs*] saying "here it is and here is Mugabe's cheque"! It was *shown* to the *Press*! So he can have a cheque to be nominated, but a ZUM candidate is turned down.'

'Will they actually go so far as to stuff the ballot boxes?'

'Well, they've done that at the previous by-elections. The people who took part in those by-elections have assured me that certain ballot boxes were brought in which they had never seen, which shouldn't have been at the count there, which were not accounted for, that it was quite clear that those ballot papers had all been folded in such a way that it was a mechanical operation. And, into the bargain, intimidation is *rampant*. At those last by-elections ZUM were not allowed to hold a public meeting. You've got to get permission to hold a *meeting*.'

'In these conditions is it actually worth taking part in the election at all?'

'Well, I think one has to because otherwise you are condoning it, but we have advised ZUM to be on their guard, that they must have their representatives at the election *sleeping* with the ballot boxes. I mean, I met a farmer in one of these by-elections where the ballot was placed in his store on his farm and there was no lock on the ballot box. I mean, he picked it up and opened it to have a look! But people *are* getting fed up, people *are* getting annoyed: people for example in queues waiting for buses at four o'clock in the morning, because there aren't enough buses, and people waiting in queues for a loaf of *bread* at four o'clock in the morning. More and more are saying "you know, this didn't happen in *Smith*'s time". But intimidation is of course a dreadful thing and a very powerful factor, and one mustn't minimise this.'

'You still seem to be amazingly popular among some ordinary Africans.'

'When I walk down the streets of Harare now I get more blacks than whites coming up to me to talk to me and shaking my hand and saying "please keep going, Mr Smith".'

'They *do?*'

'Oh yes, oh yes. And the chaps at the flower stands and the newspapers wave at me – I mean, we're even on Christian name terms – they wave and say "hello, Ian!" as I go past. If you want to see the biggest queues in Harare today, you know where you find them? The South African legation. It goes right around the street. I mean, I've counted hundreds. You will find that less than ten per cent are white. Sometimes you will see a whole row of people and you won't see one white man. They're all there to get visas to go to South Africa, to go to this "dreadful" country.'

'How come you're able to talk even to Mugabe's ministers in private? They've always seen you as the arch-enemy.'

'No, a lot of his ministers don't think that. *He* does because I had the temerity on one occasion to criticise him. That goes back nine years. That was when he started talking about bringing in his philosophy of a one-party Marxist-Leninist state. Prior to that I had seen him regularly, and he welcomed me and treated me very courteously and thanked me for giving him the benefit of my views, knowing that I represented the views of the white people. But then he started talking about this one-party state business and *immediately* there was a reaction from the point of view of the investor, both internal *and* external. People would come to see me, the financiers and the industrialists, and they said "we're not going to invest in a country that's going to become a Marxist-Leninist country." Prior to that things were positive and things were going well. So the next time I went to see Mugabe I told him that this was detrimental to our country, and I said to him, "you know, so far I haven't criticised you and I've requested my members of parliament not to as well in order to give you a good start, but in view of the seriousness of this new line of yours I have to tell you that I will have to speak in public against you if you go on like this." That was the first time I saw that he was disenchanted with what I said. I had antagonised him, and from that day on he has refused to meet me. Remembering that I was the Leader of the Opposition and there is a convention in all parliaments that the Leader of the Opposition has access to the Prime Minister, that's an indication of the smallness of the man.'

This astonishes me, this blithe assumption that a Marxist revolutionary leader in Africa should still be expected to play by the careful British rules of Westminster and Whitehall. It is probably disgracefully racist of me to expect lower political standards in Africa, but there isn't one other country on the continent, and that includes white South Africa, where politicians play their dirty game by Western democratic rules.

'Aren't you amazed, though,' I ask, amazed myself, 'that after the war, after all the bitterness that there had to be, and Mugabe had been inside for ten years, that in fact you were able to remain as the Leader of the Opposition? In a lot of countries they would have strung you up.'

'No, no,' says Smith gently, as though talking to a child. 'I'm glad you've mentioned this, a lot of people mention this, but of course this was part of the Lancaster House Agreement. There would never have been the Lancaster House Agreement if this reconciliation had not been accepted. So that would have flown in the face of Lancaster House.'

'What would have forced Mugabe to stick to the Lancaster House Agreement? He could have just ignored it.'

'No, no,' Smith chides, 'he couldn't have, because we were assured by the British (and they had the backing of the Americans and the Germans and the French) that there was an agreement and it had to stick, and it had to last for ten years before they could make any changes, and that if they violated this agreement the rest of the world would have come down on them like a ton of bricks. We were virtually given a guarantee that this just wasn't on.'

I am about to point out the world tried to come down like a ton of bricks on Smith himself when he declared UDI and it didn't do the world much good, but there is an interruption from outside the room, a message, perhaps a telephone call. He goes out to deal with it and returns several minutes later with his wife Janet tagging along behind. She tries to be bright and breezy but he seems reluctant to let her talk to me at all and is very impatient with her. When he speaks to her I am irresistibly reminded of the manner of a typical brusque white Rhodesian of thirty years ago talking to his 'kaffir' cook or 'houseboy'. Later Smith is quite happy for me to take photographs of him inside the house as well as outside, among the pink bougainvillea in the garden, but he refuses to be photographed with his wife. I wonder how much Janet Smith suffered during all those years of her husband's political career. Perhaps she is one of the great forgotten heroines of the history of Rhodesia and Zimbabwe.

I ask about Smith's recent illness. 'I'm told there were prayers for you in the Anglican cathedral three Sundays ago,' I say to him.

Mrs Smith answers: 'Well, I . . .'

'Never mind,' says Smith curtly. 'Never mind, please.'

Mrs Smith is undeterred: 'That was true. Because – I'm not an Anglican – and everybody was . . .'

'OK, OK,' says Smith.

Mrs Smith: 'But I mean, it really is.'

Smith, despairingly: 'Mmm.'

Mrs Smith's face suddenly lights up with defiance. 'He's still as stroppy as ever!' she says, and leaves the room.

'Where were we,' says Smith in a tone of deep resignation, so fed up that he says it without a question mark.

I gather my wits: 'I suppose I must ask you what the effect is going to be of the Lancaster House Agreement coming to an end.'

'Well, yar,' says Smith in that distinctive Southern African accent, 'we were talking about that and I was telling you that because of the Lancaster House Agreement, no way could they have done anything else. And in any case, what you've also godda remember is that for a long time our people were in control of the security forces. It was a gradual process bringing their people in, and if they had tried to renege on the agreement earlier on, you can imagine, it wouldn't have worked very well. But basically the agreement at Lancaster House was that we would forget the past, that we worked together to build this country, and this was an honourable agreement, a signed agreement which had the blessing of the British Government, the American Government, the French and the German Governments, we were told, so to renege on that just was impossible. That was why, whether they liked it or not, they had to go on and accept myself and everybody else.'

'But now the agreement runs out on April 18th.'

'Yes. Well, it just simply means they can change the entrenched clauses in the constitution with a seventy per cent vote in Parliament instead of a hundred per cent vote. I don't think there's a great deal they will do. Perhaps bring in this one-party state, which is what they want. Of course, that's the dream of *any* politician, isn't it, that once you're elected you stay in the government for ever. But it just means there's no freedom, and I think they're going to have difficulty because more and more people realise now, especially black people, that it's not all they thought it was going to be. I would go even further and say this to you: I think that even if they get their seventy per cent or even a hundred per cent vote in Parliament I believe that such an action is in conflict with acknowledged principles of world-accepted, United Nations-accepted freedom and humanitarian principles, and I think that any person, any voter in this country, has the right to challenge this denial of his freedom in the courts, and I think any impartial court would come down in his favour.'

This fascinates me, the wonderful nonchalant cheek of it. For fifteen years Smith himself defied world opinion and United Nations sanctions and regarded with contempt what he now calls 'acknowledged principles of world-accepted, United Nations-accepted freedom and humanitarian principles', but now he is citing them to support his own case against Mugabe and is even threatening to go to court to uphold them.

'So what would happen,' I ask, intrigued, 'if an individual

voter challenged it – say *you* challenged the one-party state in the courts, and the court found for you? What would happen then?'

'Then the Government would say "we don't accept the court's decision".'

'The courts are quite independent, aren't they, still?'

'Well, they have been pressurised on a few occasions, but fortunately we still have good judges, although sadly there are some judges who have come in and who have been appointed without qualifications and experience. Their qualification is that they have got a Party card in their pocket, and one worries how this will end up in time.'

Smith himself has recently been battling in the courts for Parliamentary backpay which has been withheld ever since he was suspended as an MP in 1987, and the judiciary has at least been independent enough to find in his favour, though the enraged Speaker of the Zimbabwean Parliament has so far refused to pay up.

'Have you actually got your money yet from your case?' I ask.

'No. No.'

'Are you going to get it?'

'I don't know.'

'The Speaker's holding out, isn't he?'

'Yes.'

'Perhaps in the new parliament there'll be a different Speaker.'

'Not necessarily. All their pals get jobs.'

Since Mugabe himself has supported Smith's claim for payment, and has behaved pretty well towards Smith and the whites, I find Smith's relentless sourness dispiriting. Isn't there *anything* good that Mugabe has done?

'I'm always open to conviction,' says Smith unforgivingly, 'but I would like to know what.'

'Nothing at all?'

There is a long pause, a very long pause. Can Ian Smith bring himself to praise Mugabe in even the tiniest way?

'I suppose he could have been worse,' Smith finally admits grudgingly, 'but I want to know what good *has* happened because people are suffering, the country's going down the drain, there's no freedom, the economy is certainly far worse than the one they inherited, there is no work for people. One of the biggest problems, a time-bomb which is ticking away here that certainly worries me and I think it must worry all thinking people, is the fact that we are turning out a quarter of a million (and I'm told it will soon be 300,000) students a year and there is no work for them. There are fewer people in work today than when this government came to power. Well, there's something wrong there. And that is in spite of the fact that bureaucracy is rampant, that civil servants have more than doubled, the security forces have trebled. In spite of that, there are fewer people in gainful employment than when the government came to power. You can't buy necessary requirements – I mean, try to buy a motor car. There are people who've had their names on the waiting list for six years. Try to buy not even a luxury car but a vanette for your farm, a tractor for your farm. You can't get them. But, as the Sandura Commission pointed out, if you're a minister in the government or a friend of the government you can get four in one month: you buy them today for $30,000 and sell them tomorrow for $90,000; at that rate you can very quickly retire in life, can't you? You can't buy spare parts for motor cars and tractors, for bicycles. Try to buy tyres for your motor car: you can't buy one, even though we've got a big Dunlop factory in Bulawayo which used to export tyres.'

I point out that for all Smith's gripes Zimbabwe is at least not an obviously rundown Third World country, like most of black Africa, but seems much more like a Second World country.

'Mozambique and Zambia are worse than here,' he admits grudgingly.

How long, then, before Zimbabwe becomes as shambolic as Zambia?

Smith hits back with relish, brandishing statistics in praise of his own white Rhodesian rule and in criticism of Mugabe's Government's performance. 'It's difficult to anticipate that,' he says, 'because they *did* inherit the jewel of Africa, they *have* got this wonderful infrastructure, they've still got a large content of white people, their skills and their knowhow. I think it will take longer than those countries, because we had a better philosophy here, we brought our black man on much quicker than those other colonial territories. I remember when I was chairman of the committee which wound up the Federation – I was then Minister of Finance – the Britishers pointed out that in this country we had roughly double the facilities for our blacks that the British *colonial* territories had in the fields of education, health, housing, recreation. I remember somebody telling me at Lancaster House that one of their colonies that had got independence had three university graduates: he said, "in Rhodesia you've got over 3000." We had already built up a middle class. We had many, many rich people, millionaires, in this country – black people with far more money than I had as Prime Minister – so we had established that base. That's why I think there is a much better chance for this country. In *spite* of the incompetence of this government, and the rampant corruption which is undermining so much, they've got this fantastic country with a great breadth of black people with skills, with knowhow, and that will help to keep it going much longer than these other countries and possibly prevent it *ever* getting down to the depths of your Mozambique and your Zambia. And there's still a large content of white people making their contribution, farmers who are amongst some of the best in the world, wonderful crops, earning foreign exchange. The majority of the farmers are still here, fortunately, because how can a farmer go? What does he do? How can he pick up his farm and go? They're prisoners, economic prisoners.'

Smith seems so utterly certain of his own rectitude and achievements that I wonder whether he would ever admit to any regrets at all, or to getting anything wrong, ever. Was there anything, for instance, that he could have done to prevent the final collapse of white power and of his rebel government in 1979?

But 'Good Old Smithy' is as sure of himself as ever. 'No, I don't think there was,' he says staunchly, 'because in the end we were never beaten by our enemies, we were betrayed by our friends. They got me into a position where I surrendered power, that was what they always wanted me to do because they could not manipulate me. But once I had surrendered power then I had lost control and *then* they started manipulating me.'

'So you were betrayed by the British.'

'Yes.'

'By Mrs Thatcher? And Willie Whitelaw?'

'And the South Africans.'

'Do you feel bitter about it?'

'No. I've always said that bitterness and hatred is a sterile thing, so I avoid that. I'm disappointed, but my philosophy is not to waste my time recriminating over the past and looking back. There's still so much to do. In spite of my criticisms of this government and my moments of despondency about our future, I still try to be positive and optimistic. We have such a wonderful country here. I love this country. It's my country, I've got no other country in the world, and so I will go on trying as long as I can to see if I can't bring back a bit of sanity to the scene, to see if I can't help to save the situation. I think that is the attitude that people must adopt and certainly I have adopted it. If people say to me, "if you have to leave, where are you going?" my answer is "I'm not thinking about that because at this stage I have no intention of leaving. It's my country, why should I leave?" But with the next breath I have got to say that sometimes when I see the happenings going on here I do pause for a moment and think, and if the situation deteriorates, if I find that my freedom is impaired, then I don't believe I could go on living here because I have dedicated so much of my life to fighting for freedom I don't think I could live without freedom. And I think one also has to concede that if the economy continues to dive down in the standard of living and the way of life degenerates to a situation where it just isn't worth going on living here, maybe I would then have to reconsider. But at this stage, no.'

I remember the bitter white veteran of the civil war who urged me to ask Smith if he still thought that his war had been a just one, if all those deaths and maimings and atrocities had been worth it. Could this be the chink in Smith's defences? The one mistake that he might confess? But of course it isn't.

'We've often thought about this,' he concedes, but then adds: 'I set up a committee on three occasions, of ministers and civil servants, to look into the pros and cons of our Declaration of Independence, and every time they came back and said we had no option, we had to do it. If we hadn't we would have just disintegrated and gone down in no time. Whereas by taking the line we did we had fifteen fantastic years here, living in a country which was one of the most wonderful countries in the world, holding the line against communism – because that's mainly what we were doing then – and creating a broad base to our economy, our industry. We had a rate of development in this country which was double what it would have been under normal circumstances. Those are *facts*, and these were points conceded by industrialists and financiers from outside. We *did* preserve freedom. We *helped* to hold the line. We helped South Africa by holding the line for so long. In all of subsequent history – what happened here, in Angola and in South-West Africa – I believe we made a contribution. It was holding back the advance of communism. This was the king-pin to this part of Africa, and if we had gone then I think it could have had serious repercussions on the history of the rest of Africa here.'

'So the war was worth fighting.'

'We believed in the end it *was* worthwhile. We had no option. I think what is important to mention is this, because a lot of people have got their wires crossed on this one: we didn't declare our independence to preserve white minority rule. That's what this government says: that's typical Marxist-Leninist propaganda. I never had an argument with the black politicians in this country. We had an argument with the British government because they reneged on the promise they made to us at the Victoria Falls conference – that was Rab Butler and that government – and because we had been promised our independence before Federation. We had been offered Dominion status. They then reneged on their promises to us. We tried for a couple of years to talk. We negotiated. I talked to Alec Home, to Harold Wilson, to all of these people, and in the end we could see they weren't going to honour their obligation, their agreement with us; and many international constitutional lawyers have told me that our Declaration of Independence was not an *illegal* act. We were simply insisting on the fulfilment of the contract made with us. The whole thing was brought about because of the British Government's deceit, and that forced us to declare our independence. It had nothing to do with an argument between ourselves and our black people, and I think it's important to stress that. I hadn't *met* any of these black people, I didn't *know* them. We never had an argument. We actually removed them from detention. Whitehead [*Sir Edgar Whitehead, Prime Minister from 1958 to 1962*] had put them into detention before we came into power. We *released* them. So many visitors to this country told me time and time again that the happiest black faces they had seen anywhere in this world were our black people. We had *no* problems, *no* political problems, *no* racial problems. *But*, after we declared our independence, of course the commu- nists then got on to the nationalists here and they offered to support them and to supply them with arms and ammunition, and they *sponsored* the war. Otherwise there would have been no war. And then tragically towards the end of that, our friends of the Free World – the British and the Americans – were siding with the Communists and supporting the terrorists in their war against us. We were a small country with a quarter of a million white people and there were fifty other countries in Africa all with votes at the United Nations involving millions of people, and that's the sort of thing which politicians think about (it's not a justification, of course): *What is going to be the most convenient thing for us to do?* And British politicians have conceded this to me, that that is what motivates them. They have been honest about it. Harold Wilson was one of them.'

Smith is a persuasive talker and much of what he says is true, and it's far too easy and glib merely to sneer at everything the white Rhodesians believed and fought for so long ago. Their ideals were by no means all selfish and shabby, and many of their achievements were remarkable. Nor were all of them racists by any means. But there's certainly one thing Smith *did* get wrong, isn't there? His remark that 'never in a thousand years' would there be black majority rule in Rhodesia. Surely that was a misjudgement. But no, not at all. Smith is still quite unrepentant. The quote, he says, was taken out of context.

'That was misconstrued,' he announces, 'and it has been twisted by the politicians for their convenience the same way as they twisted our Declaration of Independence as being an act against our black people and it was nothing of the sort, as I've explained to you. I was asked in an interview, "will you accept black majority rule? How long will it take you to accept black majority rule?" My reply was: "I'm not prepared to accept majority rule based on colour. In principle I won't accept black majority rule. I'm not prepared to accept *white* majority rule in principle." It is important to stress this as well: our franchise here had no racial bar. Blacks had access to the vote in this country the same as white people. I think it's important to stress that, because again our enemies have twisted that against us: they've accused us of having a racial constitution. It was *not* racial. It was a qualification, a very small qualification. I was often told that blacks could have come on to the voters' roll in excess of white people if they had tried but their politicians forced them to boycott it. But to get back to your question: my answer was "in principle I am opposed to a constitution and a rule based on race. I can't accept that principle. Never, never in my life. Never in a thousand years." I'm opposed to the principle of a government based on race, and I still am.'

I refrain from pointing out that this is absolute tosh: that Smith's white-supremacist government was so utterly racist that it was one of the reasons I never returned to Rhodesia. To say so would be to accuse him in his own living room of lying. But it does seem reasonable and pertinent to ask why he never had even one black minister in his government. His answer is simple, utterly credible, and might even be true.

'They were afraid,' says Smith. 'You know, intimidation is a tremendous thing here, a hideous thing. We had *some* good black people who worked with us: one very good man, I remember him at Fort Victoria, Gronda, tragically he was killed in an accident. But the blacks told me that none of them would be prepared to accept a position in government because the black politicians who were fighting us were opposed to us and they told them so in the same way as they told them to boycott the voters' rolls.'

I have one final question: a question that has always intrigued me about Smith and the British governments that he took on with such foolhardy determination and nearly vanquished.

Why is it, I ask, that he always got on better with socialist pro-black Labour politicians like Harold Wilson and Arthur Bottomley than he did with right-wing Conservatives, whom you would have thought would have been much more sympathetic towards Smith and the white Rhodesians?

'I got on better with Harold Wilson than some of the Conservatives because he was more honest than the Conservatives,' says Smith. 'We started on the basis that we were far apart because our political philosophies differed. The Conservatives told me that they were friends of mine, that we had the same philosophies, which we did, and they were the ones who betrayed us. They were the ones who gave us undertakings and went back on them. It started with Rab Butler and the Victoria Falls conference, and then Carrington at Lancaster House, who took us for a ride. I told him that what has happened was going to happen, but Carrington said: "Oh, my dear Mr Smith, we'd planned the whole thing to do the exact opposite. We can give you an undertaking that the very thing you are fearing will never take place." They accused me of being an alarmist in the corridors of Lancaster House. They said the first independent Zimbabwean Government will clearly be Muzorewa, Nkomo and Smith.

'But far worse than that: there was a clause in the Lancaster House Agreement which said "any intimidation and those people will be disqualified". There was mass intimidation: I know that; the affidavits that Soames had here when he was the Governor were in excess of 1000. And they were *going* to do something about it. Soames saw me and spoke to me about it. But three days before the election I went to see him and he said: "No, we have changed. *Peter* has told me that we won't be able to sell it to the OAU."'

Smith's tongue caresses the word *Peter* as a gourmet would taste a fine wine or a cat would sample a mouse.

His voice drops. '*Peter*,' he says, very quietly, licking the word. 'You know who Peter is?'

Of course.'

'*Carrington*,' he whispers.

Of course.

Peter Alexander Rupert Carrington. The 6th Baron: KG, CH, KCMG, MC, PC, JP, DL. And Eton and Sandhurst, of course. The British Foreign Secretary.

A dozen years of sour memories glint in Smith's good eye.

'I mean,' he hisses, 'Soames was riding under Carrington's orders, wasn't he? Who else? *Carrington* was the architect of this whole thing.'

Carrington, then, in the end, not Mugabe, is the nigger in Zimbabwe's woodpile.

Good Old Smithy! He hasn't changed at all. Even the nigger in his woodpile is still white.

CHAPTER 6

DIARY EXTRACTS

THE TELEPHONE system in Harare is wonderfully inefficient, and each time you seek the help of the operators they tell you that the call will take forty minutes, even when they connect you thirty seconds later. I try to telephone David Smith, the white Senator who has been a Cabinet Minister not only in Ian Smith's Government but also in Mugabe's. This proves difficult as his number is apparently ex-directory. '*Smith*,' I tell the ex-directory supervisor, 'David Smith. He used to be a minister in the government.' Eventually the ex-directory supervisor connects me to *Ian* Smith, who finds this more amusing than I do. The legendary Smithy is very helpful but doesn't have his less famous namesake's number. This seems odd when you think that white Harare is little more than a tiny village, where everyone seems to know everyone else, and that David Smith was once Ian Smith's Deputy Prime Minister.

*   *   *

I ask a young black Zimbabwean woman about President Mugabe and his Cabinet Ministers. 'All our Ministers are arse-holes,' she says.

*   *   *

Wednesday 21 February
PRESIDENT MUGABE'S BIRTHDAY. He is sixty-six.
I make a sentimental journey to Mutare railway station, where as a boy I would catch at the end of each prep school term the exciting overnight sleeper train home to Beira, 180 miles

away down on the coast of Portuguese East Africa (Mozambique). Those end-of-term evenings at Umtali station were
always ecstatic, after three long months of boarding school,
and as the fat old-fashioned locomotives belched steam across
the single platform, and their exotic, moustachioed Lusitanian
drivers belched garlic, the prospect of a full month of holiday
freedom and sultry days and nights beside the Indian Ocean
was enough to make any child delirious. The station is now
heavily guarded because of the war with the Mozambican guerrillas just a few miles away across the border, and it takes time
to persuade the African security guards to allow us on to the
platform to take photographs, but eventually they are begging
Laurie to take their pictures too. I wallow in an hour of sheer
self-indulgent nostalgia. The train for Harare, still painted in
the old Rhodesia Railways livery of cream and brown but now
emblazoned 'Zimbabwe Railways', is standing waiting at the
platform – the only train that day, the 21.00, and not due to
leave for another nine hours. I sit bemused in one of the
unchanged but surprisingly cramped first-class compartments,
quite possibly one of the very ones in which I travelled forty
years ago, and it smells identical today with its green seats and
pull-down bunks, its folding table and little silvery wash basin,
the frosted RR still engraved on the mirrors and windows, the
reservation numbers and letters outside on each sliding door.
For half a century this coach, made in Birmingham, has been
clattering across half a continent, back and forth, from the hot
flat plains of the Indian Ocean to the high blue misty mountains of Mutare and beyond, through sleeping jungles and
marshes and wide savannah, past palm trees and lion and
elephant, under the African moon. On the platform there is
still the glass cabinet (now labelled 'Reservations Mutare–
Beira') that I studied so eagerly on those magical nights at the
end of each term, but now it is empty. The overnight passenger
trains to Beira no longer run since the Mozambican rebels
started blowing them up. In the booking hall there are still
printed timetables giving the schedules of non-existent trains
down to the coast, but the pointed yellow sign 'Beira Train'

88

now stands forlorn and neglected in a corner like a school dunce with a pointed cap. Schoolboys can no longer catch the overnight train to paradise to wake with joy beside the Indian Ocean.

*   *   *

It's a long drive south and west towards Masvingo (once Fort Victoria) through beautiful lush countryside of baobab trees and outcrops of granite kopjes embraced by broad plains and distant mountains – a countryside so remote that I am astonished to remember that when I was fifteen I hitch-hiked alone across these vast open spaces all the hundreds of miles to Bulawayo, and that my parents allowed me to do it. It was obviously a much gentler world then.

Birchenough Bridge is still a huge, gleaming silver rainbow across the wide, sluggish Sabi River, now the Save. An odd name, Birchenough, when you look at it – very English public school. The bridge is guarded by two armed soldiers who are rare among black Zimbabweans in that they are not too keen to be photographed, but like all the others they succumb in the end. We 'lunch' at the Birchenough Bridge Hotel, which was once quite stylish and still boasts a posh sign that reads 'Lunch A La Carte 12.15 to 1.45.' But it's a dump now where the bar doesn't even have any glasses and we drink Castle beer from the bottle. The menu too looks pretty unappetising and I settle for toast and butter while Laurie chews some dreary looking sadza [*maize porridge*].

The fast tarmac road to Masvingo is enlivened by numerous truckloads of armed soldiers patrolling the Mozambique border, and by very friendly pedestrians – and optimistic hitch-hikers – who all wave and smile and give us the thumbs-up sign as we pass. In one remote bush village there is a tiny tin-roofed shack marked 'Building Society'. This too seems optimistic, since there is hardly another building in sight and the possibility of a mortgage in these wilds seems ludicrous.

Masvingo itself is still a one-horse town, one-storey, like

some forgotten settlement stranded in the American mid-west. But nearby are the sinister, towering ruins of Great Zimbabwe, the mysterious medieval stone temple and fortress that is said to house the soul of Central Africa and that may have been built by the African emperor Munhumutapa, though it has been argued that no African tribe of the time possessed the knowledge to build it and that it was probably constructed instead by Arab slave traders. Grinning black-faced monkeys scuttle about with brazen self-confidence, as though they know the answer to the riddle. The Great Zimbabwe Hotel is full, unfortunately, but we swim in their pool and have late afternoon tea beside it. A sign reads 'Monkeys are dangerous. Please do not feed them'.

Back in Masvingo we check into the Flamboyant Motel (remarkably cheap at £14 for bed and breakfast in a comfortable room with a bath). Laurie and I entertain each other in the residents' lounge by reading aloud hilarious passages in today's Bulawayo *Chronicle*, the first newspaper ever to publish an article of mine, back in 1958, when I was fifteen. The paper still carries the Andy Capp strip cartoon but is now appallingly printed, misspelt and semi-literate – and yet includes an article on the scandal of illiteracy in Zimbabwe. Everyone mentioned in it is described as Comrade, and there is an extraordinary column by someone called 'Ad Libitum', apparently aimed at youngsters thinking of going into journalism. It attacks the standards of the British Press and suggests that advertisers can bribe Fleet Street reporters by giving them 'a fine bone-china cup and saucer'. It is also claimed that Reuters ('the original from pigeon post days') is controlled by the CIA. 'So, go out there, fella me lad,' writes Ad Libitum. 'See it all, for yourself and experience the threats, cajolery, bribes, beatings, and murder all at first hand too. If you survive.'

This does not sound much like life today on the *Sunday Express*, but then Ad Libitum suddenly seems to be referring to a slightly earlier era – in fact to 1935, when apparently an unspecified British journalist was guilty of some sort of unspecified malpractice in Abyssinia. Could this be a reference

to Evelyn Waugh, perhaps? To Lord Deedes? And what do
Ad Libitum's readers make of all this in the wilds of the
Zimbabwean bush, where I doubt whether Fleet Street or
El Vino or Rupert Murdoch are general topics of conversation? And there is more to come: the 'Look At History'
column regales the readers of Masvingo with the fact that
on this day not only was Comrade President Robert Mugabe
born in 1924 but that in 1613 'Michael Romanov, son of
patriarch of Moscow, is elected Tsar of Russia, thus founding
House of Romanov.'

The Chronicle also publishes a fawning sixteen-page special
supplement to celebrate Mugabe's birthday ('A Very Happy
Birthday, Cde. President') with no fewer than twelve photographs of the great man and headlines like 'No let-up in the
pace' and 'The Midlands sends best wishes to Cde. Mugabe'
and advertisements like 'POWER SALES (POW!) Congratulate
the Honourable Cde R. G. Mugabe on the Occasion of his
Birthday.'

We also read that the Ministry of Health has just issued a
warning about the possibility of cholera in Zimbabwe, and
swiftly lose our appetites. We end up ordering the safest meal
we can think of: tinned mushroom soup, tinned fruit salad,
crêpes Suzette and a bottle of white wine, much to the indig-
nation of the dinner-jacketed maitre d'hotel.

*   *   *

Up at 5.30, and by 9 a.m. we are in Esigodini, 150 miles away,
where it is Open Day at my old public school, Falcon College,
out in the bush thirty miles from Bulawayo, where the parents
of nervous first-year boys are queuing to talk to the teachers.
The new young English master, fresh from Ampleforth, tells
me he loves the school already and is thinking of staying for
two years instead of the one he is contracted for. He says he
is amazed by the boys' rigid discipline, which is quite unlike
anything in Britain these days, but I confess that although I'm
as appalled as anyone by the slackness and impoliteness of

modern British youth, I find Falcon depressingly regimented. The boys are wonderfully polite and stand up and remove their caps whenever an adult passes, which is a welcome contrast to sloppy British teenagers, but every boy also says 'good morning, sir' as you pass and this can be exhausting when a lesson has just finished, class is out, and you pass a hundred boys going the other way.

The school and its cool, leafy avenues and colourful trees, bushes and gardens provide a magnificent oasis in the sprawl of the hot khaki bushveld and the whole settlement is very much bigger than when I was here from 1957 to 1960. It is lusher, more mature and elegant, tranquil with fountains and fishponds. It even has a proper science block and a bank of computers, televisions and videos, all undreamed of in the 1950s. But it is still recognisably the old abandoned Bushtick Gold Mine it once was, a sprawling village of scattered houses and bungalows where the old-time miners lay at night and dreamed of riches in the shadow of the nearby dusty mine dumps that gleam like vast silver ghosts in the moonlight. In my day it was very primitive, some of the houses little better than huts, and with very few facilities. The playing fields were only just being carved out of the bush and we spent many weary hours bent over them, weeding and removing boulders and stones so that now they are beautifully flat and turfed. I never felt completely at home here (the place was too white-Rhodesian and sport-orientated for my taste) but I still have happy memories of playing miniature cricket (using hairbrush and squash ball) with the fat but brilliant, swashbuckling cricketer and scholar Fred Goldstein, who had six A-grade A-levels by the time he was fifteen and went on to play first-class cricket for Oxford University, Northamptonshire and Western Province in the Cape. Fun, too, were the school plays, in which I was Bianca in *The Taming of the Shrew*, Claudius in *Hamlet*, and Jack Worthing in *The Importance of Being Earnest* – in which Gwendolen Fairfax was played by a pale, fey, frighteningly clever thirteen-year-old, Robert Jackson, who went on to become the youngest ever Fellow of All Souls, MP for Wantage,

Member of the European Parliament and a minister in Margaret Thatcher's and John Major's governments. I was less enthusiastic then about the activities of some of the young white bushmen among my contemporaries at the school, like Bruce Greenshields, who would suddenly snatch out of the air one of the large flying ants, an inch long, that used to flutter about the dormitories at night, and munch it alive, *crunch-crunch*, wings and legs and all, smacking his lips and remarking like a connoisseur that it tasted just like peanuts. Bruce had mocking eyes as green and cold as any reptile's and so of course he kept poisonous pet snakes, caressing them, squeezing the poison from their fangs and allowing them to slither all over his body. They had a habit of suddenly popping their malevolent heads out from under his shirt collar in chapel on Sunday nights as we sang hymns about the Devil. Bruce also had a taste for practical jokes: you went to bed at Falcon warily.

Still, lunch in the hall with parents and staff is jovial enough, and it is impressive to learn that Ndebele is now a compulsory language. Not one pupil was black when I was here, but now nineteen per cent of them are and they seem fully integrated and very English. The danger is, of course, that this could distance them from their own people.

*   *   *

Bulawayo, the brooding capital of Matabeleland, a modern skyscraper city where today they have a racecourse called Ascot but where a hundred years ago there stood the mud-hut kraal of the fat Matabele King Lobengula, the leopard-skinned descendant of Zulu monarchs. It's a city of bitter memories, an also-ran in the histories of Rhodesia and Zimbabwe, and the warlike Matabele tribe will surely not easily forget how they were first tricked and robbed and slaughtered by Cecil Rhodes and the white settlers a century ago, and then tricked again and slaughtered by Robert Mugabe's Mashona in the 1980s, when the Matabele were led by another fat chieftain, this time in a Savile Row suit – the Father of the People, Joshua Nkomo.

*   *   *

Harare again. At six o'clock the dawn is turning the sun in just five minutes from orange to gold to blinding white. The sky lightens to a pale blue. The dew glistens. There is a lovely fresh smell.

*   *   *

In the Grassroots Bookshop there are piles of Russian books of all sorts, stacks of Russian–English dictionaries and even a Russian biography of Cecil Rhodes. I don't suppose it is very flattering.

*   *   *

In the library of the Government newspaper, *The Herald*, a helpful black librarian searches the files for any cuttings about me, since I am told that many of my *Sunday Express* book reviews and interviews have been republished in *The Herald* and its sister paper, the *Sunday Mail*. To my astonishment he produces a huge, flatteringly bulging file marked GRAHAM LORD – but every yellowing item in it refers not to me but to Lord Graham, the Duke of Montrose, the Rhodesian farmer who was a minister in Ian Smith's rebel government. Librarians love putting names backwards, and they shun commas, so I ask for anything on LORD GRAHAM, but of course there is nothing at all.

*   *   *

At Harare Airport, as I and two other cramped passengers disembark from a tiny six-seater Cessna after flying in from Beira (in Mozambique), we are stopped by a Ruritanian motorcade of at least fifty cars with flashing lights, howling sirens, police outriders and a lorryful of armed soldiers. We are in the presence of President Mugabe and Nelson Mandela, who is making his first visit to Zimbabwe since being freed from prison in South Africa and is about to fly off to Dar-es-Salaam. A silly red carpet stretches across the dusty tarmac from the Mercedes to the Air Zimbabwe aircraft. Is all this really necessary, even in an African country with a leader who obviously suffers from an inferiority complex? Any Western leader would be ridiculed if he or she went around with even a tenth of this protection. On the other hand I suppose the traditional African respects showy display in his chieftains as a symbol of power, and Mugabe has a role to play as the reincarnation of Zimbabwe's legendary emperor Munhumutapa who has come at last into his heritage.

*   *   *

The clientèle is almost entirely black in the Captain's Cabin bar in Meikle's Hotel and they are laughing openly at the recent decision to rename the streets, one of which has been changed from Manica Road to R. Mugabe Road. 'What's wrong with Manica?' asks one smart black woman loudly. 'It's a perfectly good African name.' They are quite unafraid about expressing their opinions: this is obviously not some cowed East European dictatorship, despite all Mugabe's Marxist dreams and pretensions.

*   *   *

Outside the hotel a commissionaire – looking like some South American admiral (green uniform and cap and enough gold braid to hang any Latin American president) – is holding hands with the chauffeur of the hotel minibus. Neither is obviously homosexual. They are simply holding hands and chatting and joking as friends. We could perhaps learn quite a lot about friendliness from the Zimbabweans.

*   *   *

Over dinner one wealthy white businessman insists that Mugabe is becoming a joke even among the Africans, who are not impressed by his posturing even though they are not particularly impressed either by the rival party ZUM. He believes that this could be the beginning of the end for Mugabe's rule, since no African wants his chieftain to be a joke. It is in fact illegal to tell jokes about Mugabe but my fellow guest is bold enough to tell the latest anti-Mugabe joke – which says that Mugabe has sacked all his Presidential motorcade motorcyclists because they sit outside State House all day, revving their bikes, *Zum-Zum-Zum-Zum*. A very basic white Rhodesian joke, which is followed by an utterly outrageous allegation about Mugabe's private life. I am almost relieved he still refuses to give me an interview: this is one particular question I would not like to have to ask him.

*   *   *

To the airport at 6.15 a.m. for a day trip to Victoria Falls – an hour's flight each way and just £70 for everything, including lunch on a boat on the Zambezi. I have been warned about the inefficiency of Air Zimbabwe – about delays and bad maintenance and the lack of spare parts – and imagined that the flight would probably be on some clapped-out old banger from the 1950s, but it's a modern 707 and the flight is superb. It's another glorious clear sunny day, and it hasn't rained in three weeks except for the very first day. At 8.50 we fly right over Victoria Falls, an awesome sight with the fluffy cloud of mist hanging above the gorge like smoke. No wonder the Africans call it *Mosi-oa-Tunya*, 'The Smoke that Thunders'.

First to the crocodile ranch (why are crocs so disgusting, with those dreadful reptilian grins?) and then a long walk along the bank opposite the Falls, which are stunning and terrifying in their power, with the roar of billions of tons of misty water plunging every second over the edge of the escarpment. Even the statue of David Livingstone on the bank still looks understandably awestruck. So too are all the camera-toting Japanese tourists (yes, they get here too). The spray is so fierce that when I walk through the Rain Forest my clothes are soaked and my glasses caked, though I soon dry off in the broiling sun.

There are as many blacks as whites sipping drinks in the garden of the cool, elegant Victoria Falls Hotel, with the steamy gorge of the Falls below in the distance, and then it's a boat trip on the Zambezi with a cold lunch and eight other tourists, mainly Italians. A shy elephant on the bank. A hippo suddenly submerging with a loud gurgle. A walk on an island where tame monkeys scamper nervously along the mooring ropes on to the boat.

Later I spend an hour shopping in Victoria Falls town, where I buy a naughty present for my twenty-year-old stepson Nick: a huge 'traditional' tribesman's straw prepuce cover (OK, a cock-cosy, and one large enough to suggest that the rumour about sexy black men may in fact be true). The African women in the shop giggle helplessly when I tell them that I am going to tell Nick that it's the smallest I could find.

On the 5.10 flight back to Harare I am upgraded to first class for some reason and return in spacious splendour, though the arm-rest is broken between my seat and the neighbouring one: a delightful black air hostess chuckles that this is because it was once used by the huge Vice-President Joshua Nkomo, who requires at least three seats for comfort. There can't be much wrong with a country that can jest openly like that about its leaders.

CHAPTER 7

THE DREAM THAT DIED: SIR ROY WELENSKY

Wʜᴇɴ I went up to Cambridge to read History in 1962, fresh from the educational pastures of the Matabeleland bushveld, my tutor Andrew Sinclair (who has since built himself a distinguished career as historian, novelist, film-maker, *Times* book reviewer, and London literary lion) informed me that it was only thanks to his influence that I had scraped into the college.

He said that he had managed to persuade the college council to give me the very last History place that year.

I was of course extremely grateful and asked why he had done it.

'Well,' he said, 'there were six of you competing for the last History place and it was quite obvious from your college entrance exam papers that none of you knew anything at all about History, so we had to judge between you on the strength of your General Papers.'

'Ah!' said I, cocky as only a nineteen-year-old can be. 'Mine was pretty good, then, was it?'

'Good?' he said. 'It was terrible! You even wrote a disgraceful essay defending Sir Roy Welensky and the Central African Federation, and I persuaded the college council that you were the one of the six candidates who really *needed* a decent education.'

It's a story that much amused Sir Roy himself, now eighty-four and living in England, when I met him at his Dorset home after my return to Britain from Zimbabwe. But it's also

THE DREAM THAT DIED: SIR ROY WELENSKY

a sad story because it underlines the anti-white prejudice of Britain's liberal intelligentsia in the 1960s that allowed British politicians to betray Welensky and his dream of a properly multi-racial society in Central Africa while it still had a chance of success. Welensky's heart was undoubtedly in the right place. Despite his name (his father was a Lithuanian refugee) he was Rhodesian-born and a loyal Briton. He was never a racist. He cared about the welfare of black Africans and understood them well. He believed in educating them as quickly as possible and bringing them gradually into the political arena by giving increasing numbers of them the vote as they became increasingly capable of exercising it intelligently. As a poor-white boy, the son of 1890s bush-trekking pioneers, he had shared the Africans' poverty, leaving school at fourteen and becoming a professional boxer and railway engine driver before entering trade unionism and politics, and rising in 1956 to become Prime Minister of the Central African Federation of Southern and Northern Rhodesia and Nyasaland – an uneasy political grouping that was forced on him by the British themselves. Welensky was a democrat who dreamed of building a new non-racial British Dominion in Central Africa as free and independent as Canada or Australia. He even had black ministers in his Government who were paid the same as white members. But he was stabbed in the back by British politicians (especially Harold Macmillan) who broke their promises to him and thought they knew more about Africa than he did. Their chicanery condemned Rhodesia to fifteen years of Ian Smith's racist regime, a dreadful racial civil war, and finally Mugabe's black domination. Even after Welensky was betrayed, and stepped down as Prime Minister, he openly opposed Smith's white-supremacist policies and actually stood against Smith's party in a by-election. But his courage and vision have never been properly acknowledged or rewarded.

Today Welensky is old, sick and physically helpless and lives in English exile in Blandford Forum ('An Interesting Georgian Town' according to the local slogan) with his second wife, two teenage daughters, and a cat. They survive somehow on his life savings and a miserable Rhodesia Railways pension of £21 a week. He is not entitled to the British old-age pension and for some shameful reason he receives no government pension at all for his twenty-three years in Central African politics or his seven years as Prime Minister, despite the fact that Britain was still responsible for the federal government when it was sabotaged. 'The only man who got a pension out of the federal government was the Speaker of the federal parliament,' says Welensky. 'And of course all the civil servants. They got their pensions.' Instead Rab Butler offered him a peerage that he rejected with contempt. 'I felt too bitter at the time to accept anything that looked like a compensating factor for busting the Federation,' he says.

Sir Roy is a KCMG, a member of the Most Honourable Order of St Michael and St George, and so senior that they have given him a most honourable seat in St Paul's: which is jolly nice, of course, but a decent pension would be nicer. Eight years ago he had a heart attack in Yorkshire and Mrs Thatcher telephoned the hospital and spoke personally to the surgeon instead of just getting a secretary to do it: a typically warm and caring gesture that her successor should follow up and by telephoning Welensky's bank manager.

Sir Roy sits in his electrical tilting invalid chair in his crowded, untidy Dorset living room, pale, frail, his limbs shaking uncontrollably, surrounded by bottles of pills. He struggles to drink orange juice through a straw, with a terrible trembling, indomitably. He dreams of his beloved Africa but is determined to make the best of his twilight years and is astonishingly free of bitterness towards the British who betrayed his dream. He is also remarkably fair in his judgements of the black politicians who now rule the land of his birth and fame, making excuses even for African corruption, and he does not begrudge them their moment of glory. They too may well end their days in trembling exile like so many other African leaders.

Welensky has not lost his sense of fun. Far from it. His kind, jolly, tired old face lights up often with humour and a huge, bright grin as he tells me that he refused to have Ian Smith in his Cabinet because he was a troublemaker; that Smith was nearly arrested by the Rhodesians before he declared UDI from Britain; and that Welensky himself nearly declared UDI two years before Smith did.

He chuckles often, despite his disturbing palsy (which stops only when he sleeps and must drive him mad) and it's obvious that his forty-nine-year-old wife Valerie and their two bubbly young daughters Aletta (fifteen) and Alex (twelve) adore him.

'The one thing that really bugs me is that I'm losing my memory,' says Welensky, with a slight trace of Rhodesian accent. 'I can put up with most of the illness with a grin even though I'm a cripple and can't write, or dress myself, and have to have someone to feed me and cut my food up. But I get so bloody cross when I can't remember a single phrase that will stop me spelling out something at great length.

'My doctor was told by my consultant that this was all due to my boxing. They think that something was damaged in my brain. It isn't Parkinson's, thank God: that would be the last straw; one of my brothers died of that and I know what it's like.

'I've said to the family that if they want me to consider going to an institution of course I'll have to do it, but the family won't hear of it and I don't want to go. But it's bloody tough. Can you think of poor elderly people living on their own? I can't climb the staircase (I've got a ladder) but I have my wife and daughters. I'm lucky. I'm not a suicidal type but I've often wondered whether I would stick it if I was on my own. There'd be nothing to live for. But my wife and daughters keep me going.'

His blue-and-white suburban house – by splendid irony not far from Salisbury Street – is roomy and the secluded garden pleasant despite being infested by a mysterious biting tropical pest, the Blandford Fly (*simulium posticatum*), which he claims is more vicious than African mosquitoes or tsetse fly and which makes their lives miserable every spring. There are mementoes everywhere: busts of Cecil Rhodes and Dr Jameson; a bust of Welensky himself with a bush-hat plonked irreverently on the fine, strong head; a plaque with the federal coat of arms; a carved wooden box containing a beautiful illuminated scroll; two chairs from the federal cabinet room; nostalgic paintings of Rhodesian scenes, the Vumba mountains, a baobab tree; silver cups and trophies; drawings of himself as a young boxer and of Jack Dempsey. But this is not the house of a wealthy man. It's a Sunday, and Sir Roy is generous with offers of beer at noon and wine with lunch (white South African, of course). But there has obviously been no numbered Swiss bank account or secret cache in the Cayman Islands, which is less than you can say about certain other African leaders.

'It's quite amusing,' says Welensky, ever the optimist. 'My wife and I laugh (really, if you didn't laugh you'd cry): the pension is now £89 a month. Two months back it was as high as £98 – the Zimbabwean dollar has dropped right down. Of course I can't live on that. We survive because I used the little bit of grey matter that I had, I turned to the financial world and made a bit of money. It's not been a bed of roses, but we manage. We've got nothing to spare. We don't waste it, and we're trying to educate these two children. They go to private schools. Fortunately a friend of mine has looked after their education, an admirer of other days. Private education is shockingly expensive, but it's no use leaving them any money because you never know what happens to money: but if you give them a good education they may not make use of it but no one can take it away from them.'

Sir Roy would obviously have been desperately poor today had he not sensibly set himself up as a business consultant on trade union and labour matters when he left politics in 1963, and had he not continued to work until he was seventy-four, in 1981, when he retired to England on the advice of his doctor after suffering two heart attacks and being told that he would live longer if he moved to sea level. 'Fortunately I never placed too much reliance on politics as a way of life,' he says.

Even now, nearly thirty years after he left politics, he still receives a lot of letters: 'I get a very large mail. People write to me from all over – Kathmandu, everywhere – generally wanting signatures, and I oblige them within reason. If they're reasonable letters I make an effort to do something about it. Indians, Chinamen, you name them. Generally they start off by apologising that they can't afford to pay the return postage! But if a youngster writes and wants to learn something, if I can help him I try and do it. It's what I've always done.'

That open-hearted response is typical of Welensky, who is still (despite his financial problems) paying for the education in Zimbabwe of the two children of one of his black former servants, with funds that are still frozen in Zimbabwe. The ex-servant writes to him regularly. 'He worked for me for twenty years,' says Welensky, 'so I thought I had an obligation to do something for him.'

He is equally generous about Britain and the British even though their politicians betrayed him.

'I haven't been back to Zimbabwe since leaving in 1981,' he says, 'and I miss it tremendously, especially the weather and servants, but I couldn't go back like this, and we like England very, very much. I must admit that I've got a very soft spot for this country, principally because it believes in the things I believe in, I suppose.'

'And yet its elected politicians were the ones who stitched you up in Central Africa.'

'Yes. I still feel a bit sore about some things. Basically, what I failed to recognise was that the Empire had come to an end, and once I realised that, of course, I was able to adjust my thinking to it. But it came as a rude shock to me that we'd given up the idea of Empire. Rhodesia was intensely loyal to this country in both World Wars.

'I wouldn't say I'm happy here, but I'm very grateful for being here. You don't make new friends at eighty-four: it's very difficult indeed; there isn't the leisure here and the time for people to have the friendships that I've known in my youth. I do miss it in a way. My wife was on the Conservative Association for a short while, but you realise that there are no servants and although we've got a woman who gives us nine hours a week (she does the rough stuff) it's bloody hard graft.'

Welensky's philosophical acceptance of his plight is impressive. So too are his tolerance and lack of bitterness. He is remarkably magnanimous about Mugabe's regime even though the Zimbabwean government tampers with his mail, which often arrives in England stamped 'OPENED BY CUS-TOMS': 'I think they're searching for money because any envelope that looks a little bit fat is opened.'

But even this doesn't bias him against Mugabe.

'I never knew Mugabe, never met him, never heard of him, actually,' he says. 'I have nothing against him. I had no dealings with him at all. I think he's a man no one should underesti-mate. I think he has a lot more ability than people recognise. I think he's got courage: to do what he did do took courage if nothing else. And I think that he's showing in some ways an appreciation of the difficulties that Africa faces that lots of people are unaware of.'

I confess that I admire Mugabe for his reconciliation policy, which has resulted in an astonishing harmony between the races in Zimbabwe today.

'I'll go all the way with you on that,' agrees Welensky. 'I thought it was a remarkable bit of statesmanship. My sixty-year-old daughter [*by his first marriage*] lives in Greendale [*a posh suburb of Harare*] and she never mentions leaving Zimbabwe in spite of things being more difficult to get. There's a limit on what you can buy in the way of luxuries, there are shortages, but generally living costs are cheaper than here. The shortages are aggravating, particularly when things like toilet paper run out, but I said to someone the other day who mentioned this to me about toilet paper and was most shocked to run short of it, I said, *you know, for the first twenty years of my life I never knew anything else but good old newspaper!*'

Yet Welensky suspects that Mugabe must feel pretty insecure and cites reports that Mugabe's guards shoot at passing motor-ists who happen to make the mistake of coming too close to the presidential motorcade: 'Why do his guards shoot at people's hearts and kill them when they could shoot at the tyres and lock them up? They killed another white man the other day, a man in his forties, who wandered into a restricted area. Instead of shooting at his tyres they killed him. It's strange how Mugabe wants to show how important he is by having this retinue everywhere he goes. Whenever he goes anywhere he goes in an aircraft of his own services and he takes a whole crowd of them, and every time he leaves the airport every senior official comes out to the airport to shake hands with him when he goes.'

Sir Roy and I then spend ten scurrilous but most enjoyable minutes swapping some of the outrageous rumours that bounce around Harare as fast as a squash ball. The one that says that Mugabe is terrified of assassination after six hushed-up attempts on his life by *black* opponents. The one about the black minister who was once nearly arrested after being found in the back of a car with a white woman. And all the others, most of them utterly scandalous, about Mugabe's private life.

'I think in some ways he's a bit of a puritan,' says Welensky. 'Did you see that in the House one of his MPs likened him to Christ?'

A Zimbabwean MP had recently told Parliament in Harare that they should be grateful that God had given them 'His other son'.

'I'll say this for the Press: the Press out there didn't half give him a roasting.'

'I bet you've heard the rumour about the African witchdoc-tor who told men with AIDS that they'd be cured if they raped a white woman.'

'You know, I heard that same rumour when I was a boy of eleven. The story spread by the African intelligentsia was that any black man who had syphilis would be cured if he could rape a white child. I think it's something from African folklore.'

What about Kenneth Kaunda, the dictator of Zambia, who used to boast of his dedication to democracy and of his close Christian relationship with God (not to mention his friendship with Saddam Hussein of Iraq) but who has also managed to suppress and imprison a frightening number of his opponents and to destroy the Zambian economy to such an extent that his country is now a violent shambles? Can Zambia's plight today perhaps be blamed on the collapse years ago in the price of copper?

'No,' says Welensky, who was once the MP for Zambia's Broken Hill constituency when the country was still called Northern Rhodesia. 'In fact the copper price has never been as high as it is today. Zambia's the third or fourth largest copper producer in the world. But I think that Kaunda has in some way done quite a lot for his country and it's not been an easy job. He's done a great deal in the field of education and established the university. But of course there's the feeling of power: they must have representatives here, emissaries there, they want all the trappings of an old established government and they haven't got the wherewithal to do it.'

He is tolerant about Kaunda and Zambia even though the Zambians not only removed his honorary citizenship of the town of Kitwe but also had his effigy symbolically 'buried', complete with headstone, soon after independence.

'It's supposed to have been my grave, yeah,' shrugs Welensky. 'They did a lot of extraordinary things in the first few months of "freedom", as they called it.'

As for Dr Hastings Banda, the dictator of Malawi (which was called Nyasaland when Welensky ruled it), Welensky says: 'I rather liked the little man, actually, and weighing the balance I think that he did Malawi a lot of good.'

His tolerant attitude towards the black dictators who inherited his Central African empire undoubtedly stems from the fact that Welensky, unlike many other white colonial leaders, was never a racist and always liked Africans. 'I used to swim bare-arsed with them in the Makabuzi River,' he says. He indicates an African bust in the corner of the room. 'See that big black head there? That was a gift to me from the Prime Minister of Nigeria, Sir Abubakar Tafawa Balewa.' He chuckles. 'The black man who came down to present it to me also happened to be a very high Freemason! I've been a Freemason for a very long time, and he asked for arrangements to be made for him to attend a Lodge, and we laid it on for him!'

'I'm a Jew, of course. A poor one, actually. I belong to a Jewish congregation but I don't attend. I'm in no fit state to do that, anyway. I did attend the synagogue occasionally in Salisbury when I was Prime Minister, but I know nothing of the Jewish faith really. My mother was a Christian, a convert, which allows me to call myself a Jew, and in fact I know nothing about the Jewish faith other than that I've read the Old Testament because my father wanted it read to him in English and that's how I came to read it. There are very few Jews left in Rhodesia now. They've got a tremendous ability to sense when things are going wrong.'

Sir Roy's genial racial tolerance undoubtedly stems from the fact that as a child he lived in almost African poverty himself. His memory now may not be what it was, but his reminiscences of his poor childhood are clear and vivid and he remembers perfectly the names of men for whom he worked as a teenager and the names of the only two boxers who ever beat him in the ring.

'My father never worked in my lifetime,' he says. 'There was no dole in those days. We knew what poverty was, I can assure you of that. I get quite a lot of amusement when people talk to me about poverty. The old man and I were living at one stage in Salisbury on a standard that even the Africans would consider low. There was no social conscience, at least that we ever saw. We lived in two rooms and shared a kitchen with other people. The old man had a bedroom, I slept in our eating room, and the highest our income ever got was when I started working and the old man's income rose to £12 10s a month, of which he had to pay £3 10s rent. He had this bloody tremor as well. He'd been a hotel proprietor and trader most of his life. He was born in Lithuania in a little village outside Vilna, in Russian Poland, but he called himself a Swede because he disliked the Russians intensely. The incredible thing is that my father was born in 1843. He helped to bury the dead in the cholera epidemic of 1853, and was selling German horses to the French during the Franco-Prussian war! They got on to him and he had to make a bolt for it, ran for his life, and he went to America and had the incredible experience of voting in an election the day he arrived there! The old man was a very courageous man, because he walked up to Bulawayo in '93, and took a fancy to it, and you can imagine what Bulawayo was like in 1893.

'In some ways I think I'm like him, but he drank, and he drank brandy, and lived to be eighty-odd. He snuffed, he smoked, he drank. I've never drunk, not because I've got anything against drink but I don't like it, I like sweet things. And I've never smoked – it's not that I disapproved, I just never liked the taste.'

Welensky's mother, who died when he was eleven after giving birth to fourteen children, must have been a remarkable person too.

'She travelled up in an ox-wagon from Petersburg in the Transvaal to Bulawayo in 1894 or 1895 but before the Matabele Rebellion,' he says proudly. 'There was no man in her party, she was part of a trek of eight or ten wagons, she and her six kids were in one of the wagons. I remember listening to her talking about cooking and she told me something you'll probably laugh at now. I said: "how did you stop the meat from going off in that heat?" She said each trek had a hunter, and he shot game on the way up to feed the train, and there was plenty of game in those days, and what she used to do was to take a leg of the buck and rub it all over with fat and hang it on the back of the vehicle so that the dust would collect and settle on it, and by the time they would outspan in the evening the thing would have set solidly and you just broke it and the meat was perfect, protected by the dust. I thought it was extraordinary.

'It's amazing how one learns things about one's own family. I was trying to trace some members of my family when I was Prime Minister and I discovered in Gwelo a record that I have a sister there, a female child who died at birth and never even had a name, and no one ever told me. I was the thirteenth child and I can only remember about six or seven of them. I'm the last one still alive.'

He was born in Salisbury (now Harare) in 1907 and went to the free school for poor children, Caledonian Hall.

'I had no education,' he says, 'which is the first thing you have to realise when you talk to me. I'm bloody hopeless with maps, for instance: I can't read a map; give me a map and show me how to get to London and I'll die on the way! I was working when I was fourteen. I became a clerk for an auctioneer of second-hand books called Ikey Cohen, who was extremely kind to me. In those days second-hand books existed in the Rhodesias by the thousand, people brought them out in their luggage, there was no entertainment. He had this magnificent lot of books for sale and he let me borrow them, and I ought to thank him for the little education that I did get. I did that until I was about fifteen or sixteen. Then I worked for a dog-fancier, and then became a barman on the Shamva gold mine and on the Grand Parade mine at Sinoia. I weighed 250 lbs – no one wanted to pick a fight with me! – and I took a fancy to boxing: I thought there was fame and fortune in that direction, and by the time I was seventeen I was fighting as a pro. When you're boxing you've got to be fairly fit, and in those days they were all twenty-round bouts. The trouble was there was never sufficient competition in Rhodesia in those days and I packed it in by the time I was twenty-one because there was no future in it.

'I joined the railways as a fireman when I was seventeen, two years under age. I shovelled for four years. They eventually found out but the doctor said "you're a big strapping fellow, you should be able to do it." I'd lied but they forgave me because of my excellent record, I was told, and I went from a shunting driver on the 1st January 1928 to mainline driver in 1936, and I remained a top-paid engine driver until I retired in 1953, by which time I'd been an MP for a considerable time. The railway management hated it, of course. They granted me unpaid leave and there were spells when I never worked for three months. At one stage I was Minister of Transport and still an engine driver! Though I say it myself, I did a good job on the railways. By the time we handed over, the railways had

fund chock-a-block full of money and we owed no debts. They now owe well over £100 million, I'm told.'

'I'm told the South Africans recently gave the Zimbabweans four brand-new locomotives which they succeeded in derailing within a few hundred yards of the border.'

'I heard it was twelve,' says Welensky impishly.

One of the joys of talking to him is that his remarks are constantly punctuated by mischief. Sir Roy admits, for instance, with twinkling eye, that his first name is not Roy at all, nor even Roy-Rowland, which is what appears in *Who's Who*.

'The truth is that my real name on my birth certificate is Raphael, the name of an angel, and I didn't feel that I looked like a bloody angel. My mother called me Rowland because she didn't like Raphael, and Rowland stuck until they abbreviated it to Roy.'

Sir Roy (or is it Sir Raphael?) is particularly impish when he discusses other white Rhodesian leaders like Ian Smith and Sir Garfield Todd.

'I wouldn't have Smith in my Cabinet because I knew that he was already becoming mixed up with UDI,' he says. 'He *was* my Chief Whip but he never worked. He never did anything. He was living away, farming, and he had to earn a living in the world. I didn't hold that against him but I knew that he was on very friendly terms with the budding element in the Rhodesian Front. The truth of the matter is that there was a plan in the Southern Rhodesian government to lock Smith & Co up before he declared UDI in 1965. I don't know how far I should go in telling you this, but there was a plan to pick him up but it fell through because the Governor wouldn't play: Sir Humphrey Gibbs, a very kindly old gentleman, the last man in the world to have been there when trouble started. He didn't have that kind of make-up.'

'There was of course a strong feeling among left-wing types and Liberals that Britain should send the army in. Jeremy Thorpe talked about bombing the railway line.'

'As a matter of fact,' says Welensky, 'Harold Wilson once cried to me because I accused him of beginning to mass troops and aircraft at Nairobi, and in fact I issued instructions to knock out our airports so they couldn't land. We got to that point. And he said to me with *tears* running down his face: "Do you really think we'd have turned on Rhodesians like that?" I said: "You'd begun to collect the aircraft to do it." Some day a true account will appear on what actually happened.'

Welensky opposed Smith's declaration of UDI and is reluctant now to say much more about it ('I'm sick and tired of it, actually: one gets weary of it') but admits he had some sympathy for Smith and had even toyed himself with the idea of declaring illegal independence from Britain.

'I understood Smith's feelings but I knew he couldn't win, that was the trouble. I had considerable sympathy with him and I took no active steps to try and weaken their position, that I never tried. But we weren't living in the nineteenth century, we were living in the twentieth century. From the bloody word go, I knew. I *considered* UDI myself in 1963. The man who wrote the financial memo for me is living in this country to this day, Sir Henry McDowell. When I asked him what would be the effects of UDI he sat down and he wrote a memo for me as Prime Minister and in his memo he weighed the pros and cons and the cons added up against it.'

'Smith says his war was worth fighting, that he delayed black rule for fifteen years.'

'I think he's got his sums wrong,' says Welensky. 'He *brought it on* fifteen years earlier than it should have happened. We were working on this thing taking fifteen or twenty years for the system that Whitehead and myself were trying to introduce and which we'd begun to get off the ground: the two-tier voting plan.

'I must be fair to Ian Smith. I rather liked him personally but he was a quiet, reserved chap. I think he spoke on three subjects in the House. One was education (he was very interested in that), I think cattle was another, but outside that he didn't play much of a part and I saw very little of him. But he had to earn a living of course: parliamentary salaries weren't sufficient that he could sit back and do nothing.'

'People who've worked with him told me that he's a bit of a cold fish.'

'That's very true.'

'He claims that what he said was "never in a thousand years will I accept *any* government based simply on a man's skin colour, black or white." He claims he was misquoted.'

'He didn't claim it in those days. He was the arch white supremacist.'

'He says the only reason he didn't have any black ministers in his government was that he wanted them but they wouldn't co-operate. I don't believe that's true.'

'Neither do I. I had no difficulty in getting black ministers. I made them ministers and junior ministers and I gave them exactly the same status, housing, motor cars, pay, everything was the same.'

Sir Roy is also much amused by Ian Smith's complaint that Mugabe rigs elections by using intimidation and by delaying the publication of voters' rolls, and tells of one dubious by-election when he stood against one of Smith's Rhodesian Front candidates to express his opposition to UDI:

'The police warned me that there were threats to me and I eventually ended up with a bit of a guard wherever I went. I lost by a couple of hundred votes. They put it across me pretty well in the sense that they opened the registration of voters but never notified the *hoi-polloi*. They just failed to publish notification that the registration was open to register the voters, but their own people knew all about it. I've never been a squealer, because I don't think squealing pays, but it wasn't my idea of playing the game.'

He also says that Smith's security people tapped his telephone just as Mugabe's people now tap Smith's.

As for Sir Garfield Todd, who was Prime Minister of Southern Rhodesia when Welensky was Prime Minister of the Federation, Sir Roy is positively skittish about him (and his wife Grace) and his eyes twinkle with glee:

'Incredible fellow, Garfield Todd. I remember the skit about him: *there but for the Grace of Todd goes God!* Someone started

Union Jacks in the Vumba Mountains: the Queen Mother with head-master Frank Cary, inspecting the boys of Eagle School, Umtali, in 1953.

The Queen Mother's wine waiter: Damson Muzhange, now the caretaker at the Leopard Rock Hotel. Photo: Laurie Sparham/Network

The Bard in the bush: Eagle School's open-air theatre and the 1955 performance of *The Tempest*.

The 13-year-old thespian: Graham Lord (left) as Malvolio in *Twelfth Night* in 1956.

Daily Mail

MONDAY, JUNE 26, 1978   8p (CHANNEL ISLANDS 9p)

As horror grows over massacre of the missionaries, the message is:

WE WILL NEVER GIVE UP

By ANTHONY SMITH

THE Church whose missionaries were slaughtered in the Massacre of Umtali had a new message for the world yesterday:

'We will continue our work among Rhodesia's blacks. We will never give up.'

Eight missionaries of the Elim Pentecostal Church and four of their children died when ter-

What the West must do now—Page Six

rorists invaded the mission in the Vumba mountains near the Mozambique border.

Yesterday two of the Church's leading officials left London for Rhodesia to make sure the work there goes on . . . and to supervise the funeral arrangements.

One of them, Mr John Smith, administrative secretary, said: 'They will be buried in Rhodesia, the land that they loved.'

His colleague, the Rev Peter Griffith, works at the mission near Umtali, but was on holiday in England at the time of the massacre.

As prayers were said in Britain's 350 Elim churches, the Rev Leslie Wigglesworth, director of missions,

Turn to Page 2, Col 5

3-1

Argentina on top of the world!

From JEFF POWELL in Buenos Aires

THE Whirlwind Football of Argentina extinguished the orange flame of the Total Football of Holland last night and brought an entire nation, rejoicing, on to the streets.

The blue-and-white bedlam of the River Plate Stadium was no more than an overture to the delirious occupation of Buenos Aires by the populace.

They came chanting out of the bars, dancing down from their apartments, in from the towns and villages by cattle-trucks and 'collectivo' buses, families in their millions to celebrate the winning of the World Cup.

In their pride at staging a universally-acclaimed championship and their fever at winning it, none of them cared that football has seen more accomplished finals o' that Holland might have beaten Argentina anywhere else in the world.

The bitterness of Holland's second consecutive World Cup Final defeat — and the crowd-driven decisions of Italian referee Sergio Gonella which sent them snarling and kicking to the finish of extra time —must wait for tribute to be paid to the new god of the beautiful game.

Influence

Kempes was brought home from Spanish exile in Valencia to be the vital influence on Mundial '78, as they call the World Cup here. When the early games went by without a goal, this superstitious striker shaving off the moustache which had been his talisman in Europe.

By the last of his electrifying runs last night he had scored twice himself and creating a third Argentine goal for Daniel Bertoni to establish himself not only as the leading scorer but also the unrivalled star of this championship.

Holland, who had come into this bullring of a stadium like the loneliest men in the world, again claimed our respect for their unflinching commitment, their disciplined intelli-

Turn to Back Page

Two families . . . two survivors

Victims : Philip Evans holding Rebecca, 4, his wife Sue, Peter McCann and baby Joy, his wife Sandra and toddler Phillip. All died in the massacre at the mission. In front of this 1976 Heathrow picture are the other Evans children, Rachel and Tim, who were away at boarding school in Salisbury.

INSIDE : Crossword 10, Femail 13, TV Guide 26-27, Entertainment Guide 28, Stars and Signs 23, City 26

The Eagle School massacre: the front page of the London *Daily Mail* on 26 June 1978. Photo: Associated Newspapers

On the site of the 1978 massacre: Eagle School's Zulu head girl Glandeur Sibotshiwe and photographer Laurie Sparham in 1990.

Still fronted by a British postbox: the Umtali Club in 1990. Photo: Laurie Sparham/ Network

In exile in England:
Rhodesian ex-Prime
Minister Sir Roy
Welensky, aged 83, at his
home in Blandford Forum,
Dorset.

At home near
Zvishavane: Southern
Rhodesian ex-Prime
Minister Sir Garfield
Todd, aged 81, at his
ranch at Hokonui.
Photo: Laurie Sparham/
Network

At home in the Belgravia
suburb of Harare:
Rhodesian ex-Prime
Minister Ian Smith,
aged 71.

The new age: boys at Falcon College, Esigodini, Zimbabwe's premier public school. Photo: Laurie Sparham/Network.

The twilight of the British Empire in Mozambique: British and Portuguese officials at the presentation of my father's OBE on the Queen's Birthday at the British Consulate in Beira in 1960. My father is in the centre, my mother on his left.

Jolly British colonials in Beira in the 1950s: my father is third from the left in the back row, my uncle Jack Leckie fifth from the left; in the front row (first and second from the left) are my aunt Dorothy Leckie and my mother.

Mozambique today: the wreck and lighthouse at Macuti, Beira.

Mozambique today: the crumbling, ruined Grande Hotel in Beira, once "a symphony in cement".

started a whole host of them. One went: *It wasn't the Almighty who lifted her nightie but a lodger called Roger or Todd.* I'll tell you what I found so incredible about Todd, who is a very bright man: he was very able but there seemed to be something in his judgement that was lacking, a lack of political perspective.'

When it comes to the British politicians who finally betrayed Welensky's noble dream of a truly multi-racial Central Africa, including what are now Zambia and Malawi he is remarkably tolerant. I suspect he was just too nice and honest to be able to deal successfully with shifty political tricksters and illusionists like Rab Butler and Iain Macleod, of whom he says too kindly now that they were only carrying out the devious wishes of their Prime Minister, Harold Macmillan:

'Strange fellow, Macmillan. An odd bod. Tears would run down his face when he was arguing with me, saying that I was misunderstanding him and all the rest of it, you know, that he was with me and wanted to see the things that I wanted to see and all that bloody bull. When he asked me to have lunch at No 10 I said "No, I don't eat with people who stab me in the back." That was the very phrase I used. But there were some damned fine people, and the men that I admired included men like Alan Boyd, Lord Boyd of Merton, and Alec Home, who was a first-class man: I had great respect for him. And in the Labour Party there were men like Attlee, whom I always respected. He was a man you wanted to deal with. You knew where you were with Attlee.'

'Ian Smith says exactly the same thing about Harold Wilson. He said he knew how to deal with him but he didn't know how to deal with the Conservatives because they were always stitching him up.'

'He's quite right.' Welensky chuckles. 'We both had our fair whack of it.'

'And yet they were meant to be your friends.'

'The thing that hurt was that one was constantly being told that the Tory party were our best hope for everything and yet the people we really got on best with were in the Labour Party

– God knows why – people like Arthur Creech-Jones. I found him an honest man, and you can't ask for anything more than that. You knew exactly where you stood with Arthur Creech-Jones. He didn't try and pull any wool over your eyes. The Conservatives were doing things behind my back. For example, Macleod started negotiating with Banda when Banda was in a federal prison, behind the backs of all the governments in Central Africa, and we knew nothing about it. You know, Harold Macmillan deliberately manoeuvred me into a position when I couldn't get him on his own the time he came to Salisbury. I said "Look, Harold, you and I have got to settle certain things before you leave here," and he said, "Yes, we'll have an hour at the airport," but he did nothing of the kind. He turned up at the last moment, got on the plane, and buggered off. He was devious – oh yes – he was that all right.'

Yet Welensky is magnanimous even about Macmillan, pointing out how he must have been suffering privately under the pressures of his unhappy marriage.

'He must have had a pretty miserable life,' says Welensky, 'because he was an intelligent man and a highly-educated man. It must have been a bloody dreadful thing to have a wife who was having an affair with Boothby. I suppose the fact that she was the daughter of a duke had the influence on him. I'd have duked her myself pretty quickly!'

Welensky's lack of bitterness is the best evidence that he was never a racist, whatever the fashionable liberal English intelligentsia may have liked to believe at the time.

'I think I had the sense to realise that there was no means of stopping the continent going black,' he says. 'I've always accepted it. All I wanted was for it to be done orderly and to try and keep the good things that the white man had brought. I mean, this bloody nonsense that one hears about colonial days, how evil they were. Can you think of the buildings that Lobengula built in Bulawayo? The roads he made? The schools he established? All these things came with colonial rule.'

'And the Rhodesians were the best type of colonists?'

'They were good, actually. Generally speaking they treated their people well.'

'There was some unpleasant racism there but it wasn't everywhere. I think you should be proud of what you did in Central Africa.'

'Well, I'm not ashamed, I can tell you.'

'Do you feel that you failed?'

'I failed to achieve what I wanted to achieve, to establish another British Dominion. But we did a lot of good. There'd have been no Kariba Dam if it hadn't been for the Federation. Who would have lent either of the Rhodesias £81 million to build a lake? There wouldn't have been any Kariba Dam without me. The university was built and African education got a lot of attention and there were many good things done by the federal government. I tried to introduce a constitution that would *delay* black rule, not *deny* it. Once could only have delayed it, even if one was prepared to take up arms, which I wasn't prepared to do. We could have put up a much better show than Rhodesia did on her own if we'd had the three countries together, but it would merely have been a delaying thing. You couldn't win. It wasn't possible to win. Look at the unfairness of the South African situation at the moment. The South African government has made some remarkable changes which most thinking people wouldn't have believed were possible twelve months ago, but does it get them any credit?'

Despite his age and disability Sir Roy still looks to the future. His papers ('piles of stuff') are being catalogued by librarians and historians and potential biographers are increasingly sniffing around. 'It's becoming a bit of a bloody nuisance,' he says. 'They take up time and they ask such bloody stupid questions too. I get a lot of visitors. I only regret that I'm in the bloody state that I'm in now. I get tired. I used to be a good speaker, but not now.'

He is even half-planning to write a funny book by dictating his more light-hearted memories into a tape recorder. 'When

I came over to England I thought that I would like to write something amusing instead of the hard stuff that I'd spent most of my life with,' he says. 'There've been some damned funny things that have happened in life, you know,' and he giggles and shakes uncontrollably and trembles with mirth as he tells how his father as a young man was burying a corpse that suddenly sat up when its wrappings came loose. Welensky's memory is better than he thinks: the corpse's name was Hertz. 'Funny I should remember that,' he chuckles. 'It happened 150 years ago!'

He tells another anecdote about how his father used to babysit corpses in the Salisbury mortuary to prevent them being eaten by rats, and once again he remembers a corpse's name – 'a man called Pollock':

'The old man used to show the corpses to me,' says Welensky, chortling helplessly. 'He said "*it's not the dead ones you want to watch, it's the live buggers you've got to keep an eye on*".'

As for the future of Africa, Welensky believes that the West can best help not only by sending food but also by teaching Africans how to become self-reliant, especially in farming, instead of expecting hand-outs from other nations: 'It's got to be a judicious mixture of both, otherwise a lot of people are going to die.'

Some Westerners argue that it's a waste of time sending *any* aid at all to Africa because so much of it disappears into corrupt pockets, but Welensky is not one of them. He points out that there is nothing particularly African about corruption:

'In the financial world here there's crooked people in highly-developed institutions like the stock market, so why should you expect the black man to be lily-white from the word go? He can make mistakes too.'

If Welensky is a racist I can only say that Africa could do with a hell of a lot more of them.

When I finally get around to applying for my Cambridge PhD I know precisely what my subject will be. It will be (unlike my Cambridge entrance exam essay) a *proper* defence of Sir

Roy (or Sir Raphael) Welensky and his Central African dream. And I shall send a copy of my thesis to my old Cambridge tutor, Andrew Sinclair, who really needs some further education.

CHAPTER 8

'WE'RE ALL ZIMBOS NOW'

TWENTY-SEVEN MILES outside the fat Matabele chief Lobengula's old tribal capital, the mud-hut kraal of Bulawayo, now a busy modern skyscraper city, the podgy little Englishman who filched Lobengula's empire a hundred years ago – Cecil Rhodes – is buried in a remote, spectacular grave high in the granite rocks of the lonely Matopo Hills. It is near the site of Rhodes's last peacemaking *indaba* with the Matabele chiefs in 1896, a poignant white Rhodesian shrine of silent grandeur where only the wind whistles, with stunning views in all directions across the empty khaki bushveld where chanting Matabele impis armed with knives and assegais defied Rhodes's rifles and Queen Victoria's army so long ago. Yet was it really all that long ago?

When I was born nearly fifty years ago it was then only fifty years since my ancestors advanced across these open plains to take this land. Cecil Rhodes died only forty-one years before I was born. He was closer to me in time than my grandson is. As I stand beside his grave it is eerie to remember that tufts of Rhodes's prim little moustache still doubtless survive in the dark beneath my feet. The sun shines clear from a clean sky but I shiver in the breeze that whispers between the rocks, and in it I seem to hear the creaking of pioneer ox-wagons and the crack of whips and the cries of nineteenth-century men much younger than I, both black and white, dying in the cruel scrub and the hot, dry sand of thirsty riverbeds around about. Not far away, set deep in the rock, is the grave of that

118

other great white pioneer, Leander Starr Jameson, and just down the hill the huge monument to Allan Wilson's doomed little patrol that died so bravely in a battle with the Matabele at the Shangani River in 1893. Every one of their names is carved on the monument.

Once this spot, 'The View of the World', was a place of reverent pilgrimage for my white Rhodesian tribe – deep-voiced sunburned men in short khaki shorts and long khaki socks (with broad thighs but narrow vowels and minds) who would lope up these steep smooth granite slopes, especially on public holidays like Rhodes and Founders' Day, to pay homage to the father of the white nation. Most of those sporty, macho men would have been appalled had they known the truth: that our national hero was in fact podgy, unfit, and had a tiny squeaky voice and homosexual tendencies. Anyone suggesting such things then would have been inviting violence, for Cecil Rhodes was a white Rhodesian totem. So now, ten years after black independence, you would expect his resting place to be neglected, perhaps even desecrated – this simple yet magnificent memorial to the arch-colonial who dreamed of subduing an entire continent of native peoples to build a new British empire from the Cape of Good Hope to the Mediterranean Sea.

Yet the new black chief Mugabe and his impis have left it untouched. They have resisted the temptation to wreak Lobengula's Revenge. Not only is Rhodes's grave still tended with care, it is visited nowadays even by black Africans. Down the hill, by the car park, there is still on display a respectful history of Rhodes's life. No graffiti disfigure the vast boulders that stand, even fatter than Lobengula, as sentinels about the burial place atop the granite mountain. Rhodes lies unmolested but for the flutterings of burnt umber butterflies and the scurrying rainbow lizards that bask on his grave in the sun. Perhaps that is sufficient for Mugabe's sense of justice, for Lobengula's Revenge: for the lizards that now lord it over the founder of white Rhodesia all have blue heads, green necks, orange bodies and yellow tails – pretty close to the colours of independent black Zimbabwe's flag. The site is still marked, with amazing magnanimity, as being set aside for 'those who have deserved well of their country'. Perhaps Robert Mugabe is planning to lie here one day too beside the man whose dream he hijacked. That, of course, would be the ultimate revenge, and these silent, magnificent hills would boom with the echo of Cecil Rhodes twitching in his grave.

In many ways life has hardly changed for the white Rhodesian tribe of Zimbabwe, even after a decade of black power. Fear of Mugabe and his policies has reduced the numbers of whites from 250,000 to 80,000, and those who found sanctuary in South Africa are known derisively there as 'When-we's because of their habit of constantly harking back to the Good Old Days 'when we' ruled Rhodesia. But many who remain live like millionaires, and even the less well-off still have servants and eat egg and bacon for breakfast. In my hotel room in the Vumba (the hotel is called, of course, the White Horse Inn) there was even a paperback of Giles cartoons from the *Sunday Express*, and outside there is a croquet lawn.

Cities like Harare, Bulawayo and Mutare are trim and elegant and the roads between them are so wide, empty and well kept – and so attractively flanked by huge granite outcrops, vast sunflowers and fields of maize – that driving on the main routes, even at seventy-five mph in a small hired car, seems as leisurely and civilised as if you were gently 'motoring' across the empty countryside of 1930s Britain. African standards of dress (and their deep dislike of swearing) are old-fashioned and rather charming. Black Harare schoolgirls wear straw boaters and black mounted police clatter placidly on horseback down Montagu Avenue, even though it has been renamed Josiah Chinamano Avenue. The play being performed at the Courtauld Theatre in Mutare is set in a British Second World War field hospital in Burma, and the scenery – six red-blanketed 1940s hospital beds, mosquito nets and tinkling bead curtain – is straight out of an old Shepperton Studios war film. British credit cards are accepted almost everywhere.

Many things here are ridiculously cheap, including servants. After staying for a week in a private house in Harare I was instructed by my hostess not to tip the 'houseboy' more than £5 or the 'garden boy' more than £1.25, otherwise I would destroy the local economy. Cigarettes cost 25p for twenty, and you can send your son as a boarder to my old public school, Falcon College, the best in the country, for £1500 a year.

Other things seem cheap but are expensive in real terms because you need to multiply by about four to gauge their impact of local prices on Zimbabweans themselves since their salaries are so small. Petrol, for instance, costs £1.40 a gallon, which would be cheap in Britain but is expensive in Zimbabwean terms – the real-term equivalent of £6 a gallon. Even in the smart La Fontaine Restaurant at Meikle's Hotel in Harare a glass of wine or beer costs only 50p, roast pork and apple sauce £3.50, fillet steak £4.75, sole fillets £5. But when you multiply those amounts by four the sole fillets are costing the locals the equivalent of £20. How can any of them afford to eat out? Yet the restaurant is far from empty and many of the diners are prosperous-looking blacks.

True, some items are horribly expensive by anyone's standards. Imported hardback books can cost the equivalent of £40 and even paperbacks by Dick Francis, James Herriot and Robert Ludlum are the equivalent of £24 each. But Zimbabwean bookshops do have one great advantage: not one of them seems to stock any books by Jeffrey Archer.

At lunch at the exclusive Harare Club (where they still insist on a jacket and tie, no matter how hot it is) there are a few prosperous black faces, but otherwise it could be in Pall Mall and is full of red-faced old colonial buffers. Astonishingly the centre of attraction in the dining room is none other than Ian Smith's old right-wing minister P. K. van der Byl, who is being fêted noisily by a group of white business groupies as though he, not Mugabe, were Prime Minister. In the smoking room there is still a huge portrait of Cecil Rhodes. The Empire Strikes Back.

After ten years of black independence Mugabe has still nationalised nothing, despite calling himself a Marxist: 4000 white farmers still own thirty per cent of the arable land; 800,000 black peasants share another thirty per cent. In salubrious suburbs of Harare, like Greendale, rich whites live in magnificent houses, with acres of glorious lawns and swimming pools and gardens bright with scarlets and mauves, that would cost £1 million or more in Britain. In Zimbabwe you can buy them for £200,000 or less – or as little as £80,000 if you're prepared to take a chance and change your money on the black market.

When I went for dinner with one elderly couple the servants were still wearing white uniforms, red fezzes, red sashes and white gloves, and the meal (soup, roast beef and Yorkshire pudding, apple pie and cream, four cheeses, good wine) was served with elegant silver, cut glass and real old colonial style. One forty-eight-year-old guest, a school contemporary of mine who has three servants and drives a Volvo, boasted that his *main* job (working for a foreign aid agency!) earns him £100,000 a year (in a country where graduate public school teachers make only £3000 a year) and he is also involved in several other businesses. Those of my old school acquaintances who stayed on in Zimbabwe after independence seem to have made piles of money. One of them, my good old friend Ian Ehlinger, never passed an exam in his life and I remember worrying about his future when we were teenagers, yet now he runs the botanical gardens at La Rochelle, near Penhalonga, and lives in a beautiful rural setting in a large manor house, once owned by Sir Stephen Courtauld, with a swimming pool, broad lawns, and a staff of twenty gardeners and servants – the sort of place where lizards loiter on the walls in the sun. I, with my Cambridge degree and comparatively high-powered London job, live in a tiny modern box in polluted Fulham where I empty the wastebins and wash the dishes.

An extraordinary example of white survival in Mugabe's black Zimbabwe is David Smith, who was not only Ian Smith's deputy Prime Minister but also went on later to serve Robert Mugabe for two years as Minister of Commerce, Trade and Industry – one of only two whites to survive in government after the transition to black independence – and then to be appointed a senator. David Smith is a big, bluff, sixty-nine-year-old Scots farmer and businessman, a friend of Sir Laurens van der Post, and lives in enviable style almost next door to Mugabe's State House. He has a chauffeur and a red Mercedes Benz, thus qualifying as a white member of the local 'Wa-Benzi' tribe. The Mercedes is not the only visible sign of his wealth. At a time when most Zimbabwean whites have to scratch around for the odd £100 of foreign currency if they want to leave the country on holiday, he and his wife travel abroad often. He seems to have as many fingers in as many pies as Little Jack Horner, including the plum building society CABS and the Beira Corridor group, and is still a crony of Mugabe's. He lives in a spacious, elegant house with a big colourful garden, portable telephone, video, and a huge television set. It is just the two of us for lunch, and his black servant wears white gloves and serves smoked salmon, lamb roulades, tiny potatoes and peas, and an immaculate soufflé that is still rising as it reaches the table. We drink excellent wine, and plenty of it, but sensibly David Smith refuses to speak to me on the record, a canny reticence that may help to explain how he has prospered for so long. David Smith is a survivor.

He and many other prosperous (and obviously powerful and influential) whites in Zimbabwe make you wonder whose body is really lying in Cecil Rhodes's grave up there in the Matopo Hills. Can Rhodes really be dead, when his legacy of white supremacy is still so apparent? Is it really the blacks who are running this country? When I watched some of the dreary First 'Test' between the Zimbabwe and England A cricket teams, at the Harare Sports Club, it seemed almost inevitable that the only black man in either team was English, David Lawrence – and one of the Englishmen batting was called Rhodes.

Out shopping in Harare with a friend, I was astonished when she said to a black shop assistant: 'Haven't you got a sunhat for this boss?' *Boss*? I had expected words like 'boss' and 'boy' would by now be long taboo, along with derogatory terms like 'kaffir' and 'munt'. The Africans have been in power for ten years but it still feels like white Rhodesia – at times uncomfortably so. In general Zimbabwe is an oasis of racial harmony, but racism is not dead.

In one mainly white bar one of the drinkers made a typical old white Rhodesian joke when he asked me: 'What do you call a black accountant? An embezzle-*munt*.' He and his friends spoke quite openly and disparagingly of Mugabe as the silent black barmen polished the glasses and listened with dark darting eyes. Another old-timer chuckled with contempt when he told me that Kingsway in Mutare had just been renamed Chaminuka Way: 'Chaminuka was a spirit medium,' he said, 'who foretold the arrival in this country of men with no knees – men in long trousers! This appears to be his only claim to fame.'

To be fair to these disgruntled whites, though most things still work well here – electricity, fresh water, hot water, and so on – there are deep pockets of chaos and inefficiency. It can take nine months to get a passport and public transport is a shambles, especially the railways. Three months ago one businessman despatched by rail 65,000 tons of fertiliser for Zambia that should by now be in the ground producing next year's crop: it is still sitting in a siding near Victoria Falls. The West Germans, realising that in Zimbabwe the problem is bad management rather than famine or poverty, have now given the country $1 billion-worth of aid not in cash but in management man-hours, believing that the system must be put right before it's worth investing in any hardware.

There are of course always disgruntled whites who never stop complaining. The telephone system is particularly erratic and in one hotel, after spending a frustrating hour hanging around the reception desk trying to telephone London, I remarked to another white guest who was also trying to make a call: 'Well, there's *one* thing that doesn't work properly here – the phones.'

'*One* thing?' he said viciously. '*Nothing* works in this fucking country.'

He has obviously never been to Zambia or Mozambique.

He and his friends spent the entire evening getting drunk and loudly finding fault with almost everything, until eventually the black head waiter was slinking in and out of the dining room, trying to avoid their attention.

To be fair, it is not difficult to become irritated with some aspects of life in Africa, and Zimbabwe is no exception. Complain about anything at all and the black Zimbabwean involved will look you in the eye and announce: 'I Am Not The One.' This is the time-honoured Zimbabwean excuse for any sort of cock-up.

At our hotel in Masvingo (which came complete with four black hookers in the bar) the restaurant was ridiculously pretentious, with the *maitre d'hôtel* wearing black tie and dinner jacket and wielding a flaming pan and a gas bunsen burner. But when I tried to sleep, and found it impossible to switch off the radio in my room, the reception clerk promised to send someone immediately to disconnect it but no one arrived. In the morning Laurie Sparham told me that he had been standing by the reception desk when I telephoned and the clerk had blithely written down the wrong room number, so that some poor baffled blighter in Room 56 was probably roused in the middle of the night by a mysterious visitor announcing 'I fix your radio'. If the sleepy guest had protested he would undoubtedly have been told 'I Am Not The One.'

Some black Zimbabweans in positions of small authority can take themselves very seriously, especially if they have been promoted beyond their levels of incompetence. The hotel manager who kept trying and failing to connect my call to London was magnificently lofty, refusing either to accept any suggestions about the correct code to dial or to let me dial it myself. When eventually he deigned to listen we made the connection quickly. A couple of hours later, just before midnight, I went downstairs to the bar for a beer before bed and found him smuggling into a darkened hotel a cowed tribal black woman and her daughter. His wife and child? Probably not: more likely his young mistress and her mother. Whoever they were, they were obviously not meant to be there and the snooty manager's embarrassment was wondrous to behold. His pomposity suddenly deflated, and he was deeply confused when I asked to sign a chit for the beer since the till in the bar was now locked.

'What is the date?' he enquired, shooting his cuffs and glaring at the alarmingly empty spaces on the bar chit.

His women simpered in the shadows.

'The twentieth,' I said.

'Ah, but you leave tomorrow?'

'Yes.'

'The twenty-first.'

'OK, make it the twenty-first.'

He looked at his watch. It was now 11.57 p.m.

'No, it is not yet tomorrow,' he said, frowning. 'It is the twentieth.'

'Fine. I'll sign it for today, then.'

He gazed at me with gratitude. Suddenly the world made sense again. He nodded briskly. 'Very good. Yes. It is not yet tomorrow.'

By the time he had filled out the chit, and I had signed, it was just after midnight.

He glanced at his watch again, and opened his mouth.

'I Am Not The One,' I said. 'Goodnight, ladies.'

But these are small irritations. More seriously many businessmen, who have to wrestle every day with the infuriating problems of trying to make things happen in Africa, have genuine complaints about the endless delays, bureaucracy, shortages of spare parts (and goods like clothes pegs, toothpaste and matches), the sixty-five per cent tax rate, and especially the restrictions on currency export and foreign exchange.

One elderly couple who live in great luxury nevertheless complained: 'We're trapped, especially pensioners like us. Trapped in Paradise. Even if we decided to leave the country and sold up everything we'd still have to invest it all in government stock at just four per cent interest. When we go abroad we're like beggars. We have to scrounge off friends and relatives. No one likes being a scrounger.'

It is difficult not to sympathise, even though they live much better than most Britons – and a damned sight better than ninety-nine per cent of their fellow Zimbabweans – and their wealth has been built on the exploitation of cheap black labour. The price they are having to pay now seems sadly just.

Even so I felt particularly sorry for some of the poorer, very elderly white old-timers, like the delightful eighty-eight-year-old man who lives on a tiny pension in a shabby bungalow that he says is worth no more than £10,000, and the sweet but frail little eighty-nine-year-old widow living sparsely in a tiny flat. They seem indomitable, these ancient Britons, themselves almost pioneers and born before Cecil Rhodes died. Their Zimbabwe has changed beyond all recognition, but they never complain. They seem to be descendants of a different tribe.

The greatest white complaint is about the widespread corruption. 'Zimbabwe gets hundreds of millions in foreign exchange and aid, but where does it all go?' I was asked by a twenty-five-year-old white Zimbabwean who has now decided reluctantly to live and work in South Africa. 'This is a great country but it's going down the drain economically and will end up like Zambia.'

One white local government official told me that although the main roads between the cities appear to be excellent they have not been properly maintained and will all crack up next year after the recent record rains. He said too that despite all the rain Bulawayo is about to have water rationing because of government inefficiency.

Even some of the young white liberals are leaving. One couple who could never be accused of racism told me that they are both so disillusioned that they are emigrating next year to Australia, and a man who has lived here for twenty-six years told me he was thinking of going to Czechoslovakia, of all places. An experienced local journalist believes that Zimbabwe will begin to collapse seriously in 1992, and cynicism among whites is rife. Many of them don't even bother to re-register to vote in elections since this can mean queuing for hours, and they claim it's a waste of time anyway because of electoral corruption. Many of them will happily lend you as much local currency as you like so long as they are repaid illegally in sterling in Britain. The richer whites hire all-night guards to protect their property, and a leading politician told me that crimes like mugging and rape are increasing alarmingly.

The fact that the white millionaires and Fat Cats have now been joined by a few rich black businessmen and politicians (who may not owe their new wealth entirely to honest hard graft) probably explains the racist bitterness that still infects some of the poorer whites, the lower-middle-class clerks and functionaries who suddenly seem to have been by-passed by history. As young men twenty years ago they could still aspire to the middling jobs which would bring them the big swimming pool, the three cars, the five servants, but now in middle age they have no hope of more than the small swimming pool, two cars and one servant. Their jobs are no longer as safe as they were, and hopes of promotion are threatened by the policy of Africanisation: racism today in Zimbabwe works both ways. Their children are disillusioned and emigrating, but they themselves simply cannot afford to leave: they would lose almost everything – and they blame it all of course on Mugabe and the 'munts'.

One late afternoon at Mutare Sports Club I was watching the England A team playing cricket against Young Zimbabwe. It was an idyllic scene, so English, with shadows lengthening across the deep green turf and small boys of all races mobbing the black English bowler, David Lawrence, for his autograph. All of the boys were wearing school caps until one brown child remembered his manners, and muttered to the others, and all the caps were suddenly removed, surreptitiously. And then the idyll was shattered when a drunken white spectator suddenly assaulted a black man, swearing loudly, scattering chairs, and had to be dragged away by two other whites. Who can guess what racial tensions still simmer beneath the placid surface of modern Zimbabwe?

But it is not only lower-middle-class whites who still exhibit a deep bitterness about black independence. At one dinner party in Harare I was astonished by the vitriolic views of two white couples who have done pretty well for themselves since Mugabe came to power – a politician and a farmer and their wives. One of the women even boasted of being a born-again Christian, yet she was as racist as the most outspoken of Ian Smith's old right-wing Rhodesian Front, who used to think nothing of comparing blacks with baboons. Throughout dinner this foursome kept running down the 'munts' and 'kaffirs' and were contemptuous of the black man's ability to run anything at all in Africa. Much of what they said was probably true, and African inefficiency can indeed be immensely irritating, but it was their viciousness that startled me. I asked the born-again Christian how she could talk like that and call herself a Christian. She was bewildered: she simply could not understand my argument. It was as though she refused to believe that black men too may have souls. For her God is still a white Englishman.

It was a depressing evening, especially since I am not a bleeding-heart British liberal who believes that everything black is good and everything white is bad. Indeed, I had several arguments with my photographer, Laurie Sparham, who seemed contemptuous of almost everything white and to glamourise anything black. Laurie is thirty-eight, and looks like Hollywood's idea of a trendy Press photographer in his fashionable chinos and fisherman's jacket (all those useful pockets) and probably reads *The Guardian*. So we did not always agree. When we helped an African hitch-hiker by giving him a thirty-mile lift into Bulawayo, and he directed us far out of our way for his own convenience, making us late for an appointment – and then even persuaded me to knot his tie for him before he left the car – liberal Laurie just laughed, and I can see now that it was funny to be conned so blatantly. But on another occasion, when we gave a lift to a nice young black couple and went willingly out of our way to drop them in the centre of Bulawayo, again making us late for an appointment, the hitch-hikers were very grateful, but Laurie, typically, kept thanking *them*, as though they had done us some favour. He was much given to fawning over Africans, touching them, patting them, putting his arms around their shoulders, in an extraordinarily condescending manner that he would never dream of adopting towards a European. To me his attitude seemed patronising and I told him so, pointing out that it is just as insulting to fawn over a man because of his colour as it is to discriminate against him because of it.

But however much Laurie and I differed, we would have agreed about that dreadful dinner party with the racist foursome in Harare. It was horribly revealing. So too was the hour we spent in a bar one evening chatting with a typical white Rhodesian 'red-neck', a short, stout middle-aged man with a ruddy face, white hair and moustache, and twinkling eyes, who boasted about his military role in Ian Smith's war and said proudly, without shame or regret: 'It was great: 250,000 of us held the whole world at bay, but we ran out of people.' Even so he kept calling Mugabe 'Bob' and preening himself because he and several local white farmers had just been asked by Mugabe's ruling ZANU-PF party to play a bigger part in advising the government on local affairs. 'We're adaptable, man,' he announced airily. 'We're all Zimbos now.'

For one surrealistic moment I thought he had said 'bimbos'.

Liberal Laurie could bear this no longer. 'You've been bloody lucky,' he said. 'Anyone other than Mugabe would have chucked you out of this country years ago and you'd be living today in a terraced house in Woking.' I agreed with Laurie then too.

The whites who will survive best in the Zimbabwe of the twenty-first century are those who are prepared to forget the past hatreds and to roll up their sleeves and work with Mugabe and his successors, whatever their faults. One immensely rich, influential, elderly white businessman who lives in great style in Harare (even though he was once a staunch supporter of Ian Smith) told me that he was always against Smith's UDI; that the civil war should never have been fought because it caused too much death and misery; and that in any case full African independence was always inevitable and even Smith's predecessor as Prime Minister, Winston Field, had privately admitted it. He knows Mugabe well, and regrets his desire for a one-party state, but points out that the whites can hardly complain about a one-party state since Rhodesia under Ian Smith was also a one-party state. He admits that his own comfortable life is a lingering relic of the old Rhodesian style, and that although he still makes his black servants stay on until midnight if he wants, the younger generation of whites now send their servants home at 5 p.m. He is one of the last of a dying breed, a personification of the twilight of colonialism and the British Empire, but for him there are no regrets. He has adjusted, and done remarkably well because of it.

Few Europeans are prepared to go as far as to join Mugabe's ruling party, ZANU-PF, and to help shape the political future, but one who is actually in Mugabe's Cabinet (one of three white ministers) is Denis Norman, the most extraordinary white survivor of them all.

Norman is not only a big businessman and farmer (and ex-president of the Farmers' Union) but was also an elected senator in the black Parliament and one of Mugabe's rare white ministers in his first government (he was made Minister of Agriculture when Mugabe came to power in 1980). In 1990 he became Mugabe's new Minister of Transport and National Supplies, a month after I spoke to him in Harare at his Tabex offices, which were once the old tobacco auction floors where the babbling white Rhodesian auctioneers could beat the world record for gabbling incomprehensibily and would sell bales of tobacco in seconds.

Norman is extremely genial, approachable, helpful, and optimistic about the future of Zimbabwe.

'Mugabe is intelligent, very articulate, pragmatic, and has great integrity,' he says. 'I have enormous respect for him. He's performed an amazing balancing act and he has such charisma that it would be sad for Zimbabwe if he relinquished power soon. He's not at all evil or bigoted, and I'm not even sure how much of a Marxist he is any more. I see him a lot, and he always says: "Judge me by my actions, not my words." He told me that he inherited a mixed economy and that until he found something better he'd better make the best of it.

'He's a very closed man, a listener and thinker, and he doesn't hear enough bad news, though I try to tell him. You can get isolated in his position, but I'm optimistic about the future. If we were going to become like Zambia it would have happened already.'

Norman says that he was always opposed to Ian Smith's Rhodesian Front party and that a lot of the old white fears about Mugabe have proved to be unfounded: that although there has been an exodus of white doctors, accountants and lawyers (and despite the Africanisation policy that has blocked promotions for some whites) most Europeans in the major industries (agriculture, mining, commerce) have stayed, if only because it has been difficult for them to leave without losing everything: 'To a certain extent they're locked into the system.'

'There's been an eighteen per cent reduction in the numbers of white farmers,' he says, 'but we were becoming a sort of geriatric society and now their average age is down from fifty-three to thirty-eight. We're now reaching the second watershed of Zimbabwean independence. It's ten years since independence but the government has still not nationalised any industry or property and it has honoured every debt and all pensions (which cost £23m a year) and every clause in the constitution.

'That doesn't smack of Marxism-Leninism. This is a very responsible government with a good track record. The basic structure works. We have good roads, banks and stock exchange, and we're self-sufficient in foodstuffs. We're not really Third World at all. And I don't believe things will go wrong. The key is the economy, which I think they'll liberalise in the next budget. They've already relaxed a bit and are liberalising trade. In ten years' time this will be a prosperous part of the world. We're playing the final act of liberation, and Southern Africa has huge resources of power, minerals and food.'

Norman doesn't pretend that everything is wonderful.

'Only 52,000 African families have been resettled in ten years instead of the promised 162,000 in three years,' he says, 'so the government has not kept to its target. They've got to resettle more and provide more back-up and support services, and they should decide what crop to promote in which area and to provide a decent infrastructure, marketing help, training and agricultural institutes.

'The biggest problem is unemployment. There are 100,000 school-leavers each year but only 10,000 new jobs at the most. There's dissatisfaction among the young, with riots on campus and the government closing the university last October until April. And we *must* have new industry, investment and labour regulations. For instance, you just can't dismiss anyone at all. It's illegal to sack anyone except for dishonesty, and even then you need permission from the Ministry, and that's a major constraint. It would be more sensible to have at least the right of *replacement*.

'Another problem is price control. And there's still quite a bit of tribalism within ZANU-PF, and there's a lot of corruption: five ministers were sacked, and one jailed – and then Mugabe pardoned him. But our judiciary is very straight.'

The general election will be 'reasonably fair' (whatever that means) but Norman (an ex-senator himself) admits that he is 'a bit sore' about Mugabe's abolition of the Senate and points out: 'A second Chamber provides a very useful service. It's so easy to pass legislation on a wave of emotion, and there may be certain clauses that need altering, and although the second Chamber can't make changes to legislation it can delay it and refer it back. Without it, who's going to act as a filter mechanism? It's a pity to lose the Senate: all legislative systems need a checking mechanism.'

Even so, he dismisses the fears (of both blacks and whites) that Mugabe's unrestricted powers after the 1990 expiry of the Lancaster House Agreement will free him at last to set up a one-man dictatorship and one-party government tyranny. 'They'll be tougher on absentee landlords and investments,' he predicts, 'but not on the white working farmer, who will have nothing to fear. I don't think Mugabe will legislate for a one-party state.'

And what of the place of whites in the future in modern black Africa?

'It's no good us sitting carping on the sidelines,' says Norman firmly. 'The whites who have stayed are prepared to make a go of it.'

Even Cecil Rhodes, I suspect, would have agreed with that sentiment. He too was a man who believed in making a go of it, and despite the shift in political power in Zimbabwe from white to black his inheritance is still astonishingly intact. I would not be at all surprised if on moonlit nights his ghost still grins among the fat grey boulders of those mountains of the Matopos.

PART TWO

MOZAMBIQUE

CHAPTER 9

'THE SEWER OF AFRICA'

IF ZIMBABWE is still the Jewel of Africa, not a Third World nation at all but surprisingly civilised and efficient despite ten years of black independence and blatant nepotism and corruption, then Mozambique has now sunk into the desperate bottom league of the Fourth World. It has become a stinking slum.

You wouldn't guess it by the stylish appearance of the Mozambican Embassy in London. It's in Fitzroy Square, in a quiet, elegant house with a blue plaque on the wall announcing with delightful irony that it was once the home of the decidedly un-Marxist Lord Salisbury, the Victorian Prime Minister after whom the arch-imperialist white supremacist Cecil Rhodes named the capital of Rhodesia. The dapper little black Mozambican diplomats issuing visas in what was once Lord Salisbury's drawing room have probably never heard of him, let alone of Cecil Rhodes, but they behave with punctilious Victorian politeness. 'I must apologise for all this irritating bureaucracy, Lord Graham,' says one smart official in an Oxford accent and what looks like a Savile Row suit. His gleaming shoes whisper against the new wall-to-wall carpet. 'I'm afraid I must send your details to Maputo first for approval. By fax machine. It may take as long as a week.' Fax machines? In Mozambique? I had been warned that it might take months to get a visa. He smiles politely. I point out reluctantly that he is mistaken and I am not in fact an aristocrat despite my Aquascutum suit. He seems disappointed. 'Graham Lord?' he says wistfully, 'not Lord Graham?' So much for Mozambican Marxism in 1990.

*

In 1987 Mozambique was named in a Human Suffering Index report as the most miserable country on earth, more desperate even than Ethiopia. It has the worst infant mortality rate in the world – eight per cent of under-fives – and millions of Mozambicans are starving. I couldn't believe the report when I read it – not only because the very name Mozambique conjures up exotic Indian Ocean images of perfumes and spices, silks and satins, of dhows creaking with silver and gold from King Solomon's mines, but because I remember vividly how idyllic it was for a child to grow up on the white-beached, palm-fringed shores of the Indian Ocean and how stylish Mozambique had been under the influence of the British and Portuguese in the 1940s and 1950s.

My part of Mozambique, the district of Manica and Sofala and its capital, Beira, was all but a British colony until 1947 when the pukka Mozambique Company handed it over to the Portuguese. It was through Beira that Cecil Rhodes first arrived in Rhodesia, in 1891, and he was furious that he failed to annex it to give his colony a vital link with the sea. The Mozambican newspapers and currency were English. Cars drove on the left. Hundreds of Britons ran the docks and railways, sweating in white suits and pith helmets in 110 degrees and hundred per cent humidity in the wet summer months. In Beira (later famous in the late 1960s as the oil port blockaded for years by the British Navy to prevent fuel reaching Ian Smith's rebel Rhodesia) my father was general manager of a British shipping firm, the Manica Trading Company, that had been granted a charter by Rhodes 'to exploit the kaffirs' in 1892. My father's work there from 1928 to 1960 earned him a proud OBE, especially his efforts during the Second World War, when Beira was a neutral nest of Nazi spies and the German battleship *Graf Spee* was cruising with sinister ease off the coast in the Mozambique Channel before sailing away to South America to meet her end at the Battle of the River Plate; when Malcolm Muggeridge was a British agent just down the coast in Lourenço Marques, now Maputo, and became so depressed by the place that he tried to commit suicide by swimming far out towards the black night horizon of the Indian Ocean before changing his mind and swimming back.

The British in Beira then played cricket and croquet, and soccer and tennis at the Amateur Sports Club, where coloured fairy lights swung gently in the muggy breeze on the creaking wooden evening verandah, where the annual highlight was the cricket match against Freddie Green's team from Salisbury and where my father edited the club magazine in the 1930s. They played golf beside the Chiveve Creek on a coarse eighteen-hole course where huge crabs scuttled out of the rough, each waving one large red claw, and kidnapped the golf balls; where a crocodile was once spotted sauntering across the eighteenth green; and where once, in a scene worthy of P. G. Wodehouse, a lioness upset a careful niblick shot by emerging from a bunker. To water the parched turf the members flooded the golf course two feet deep and held a regatta. They giggled at fancy dress parties. They played billiards under huge lazy fans in the Beira Club, and read the results in the *Beira News*, and the British wives played a game of Edwardian etiquette by calling on each other in turn and leaving visiting cards with the corners folded over just so.

They watched with full hearts the flying-boats from 'Home' landing on the Pungwe River, and sang *Jingle Bells*, and on New Year's Eve they waltzed until dawn in wilting starched collars and damp dinner jackets at the old Savoy Hotel to Ruby Maclean's band and the amazement of African waiters in monogrammed uniforms and red fezzes. One of the main squares was called Piccadilly Circus. And for years my father's stifling office near the docks was cooled by an old African punkah-wallah called Funny-face who lay half-asleep in the sandy yard outside and kept the office fan moving by waggling it to and fro with a long piece of string connected to his big toe. Somerset Maugham and Graham Greene would have understood.

There was in those days a delicate Portuguese flavour of elegant mosaic-tiled villas and colourful gardens, of tree-lined avenues, squares and fountains, of evening families promenading past the busy pavement cafés, of stylish Portuguese bullfights where the bull was never killed.

So when I read of the Human Suffering Index report I was saddened and bewildered. How could this place of such happy memories have become the most miserable nation on earth?

Fifteen years of incompetent black independence and Marxism have done it, and teams of Soviet 'advisers', and a meagre economy based on cotton, prawns and cashew nuts, and a crippling civil war with the anti-Marxist Renamo guerrillas. A week before I went to Beira in 1990 terrorists ambushed and kidnapped a forty-six-year-old British hydrologist, Professor David Stephenson, and a forty-year-old Zimbabwean construction firm director, Dudley Searle, when they made the mistake of driving down from Mutare along the dangerous terrorist-infested Beira Corridor road instead of waiting for a plane. 'Whatever you do, don't drive down to Beira,' I was warned by the Foreign Office in London and by our embassy in Maputo, even though Mozambique has at last rejected Marxism and is encouraging capitalism, tourists and Western investment and British soldiers are training the Mozambican army. The Renamo rebels, apparently no longer funded by the South Africans but by disgruntled exiled Portuguese businessmen and landowners determined to reclaim the wealth they abandoned fifteen years ago, are still blowing up the oil pipeline to Zimbabwe and derailing the trains. The exotic Beira overnight sleepers and grunting steam engines that used to carry me to and from my schools in Zimbabwe no longer run. The down-train platform on the Zimbabwean border at Mutare station is deserted, the passenger trains have been cancelled, and excitingly alien pistol-toting Portuguese customs and immigration officials no longer board the air-conditioned coaches at Machipanda with their snug holsters and smug epaulettes, their swarthy moustaches and garlic breath and reluctant rubber visa stamps. Beira schoolboys can no longer wallow in the glorious end-of-term excitement of waking in the jungle at 5 a.m. on the overnight train to the coast and sniffing the early morning whiff of tropical marsh, of dried animal hides in the warehouses at Munhava, of coconuts and the tang of the distant salty Indian Ocean. No longer can they relish the joys of approaching home across the flat veld at last by rail, crossing the high wide span of the sultry Pungwe River bridge at dawn and lobbing stones at the sullen crocodiles basking far below.

This time instead I flew in to Beira from Harare in a tiny six-seater Cessna, bouncing low on cloud and praying that we were out of sight of any enthusiastic guerrilla Sam missiles on the ground. Fuel in Beira is so short that we had to leave one suitcase behind. I wished we had jettisoned instead the fat red-faced South African businessman sitting opposite me. He seemed too heavy for such a frail aircraft and our cramped knees kept knocking – or maybe they were only mine. He slept all the way and snored with Afrikaner arrogance. When finally we landed at Beira, the Cessna a wobbly insect buzzing out of the sky, the heat was like an opened oven, but I understood only too well why the Pope kisses the tarmac whenever he arrives safely somewhere new. 'Do you make this trip often?' I asked the young South African pilot, who looked about nineteen. 'I haven't done it for years,' he grinned. At a moment like that the tarmac of even Mozambique looks extremely attractive.

'You can gauge a country's health by its potholes,' I was told by the Associated Press's correspondent in Harare, John Edlin. If that's true, Mozambique is very sick indeed. They still drive on the left-hand side of the road but the potholes are big enough to lose a cat and the open manholes reek with the stench of effluent. Beside the old beachside Oceana Tea Rooms, just yards from where black children splash and squeal with delight in the shallows, a fat sewer runs straight into the sea. The atmosphere is as dense and pungent as a simmering bowl of faeces. It seems wiser to smoke than to breathe.

When my father first sailed from London to Mozambique in 1928 on one of the old Union Castle mailboats, the *Gloucester*

141

Castle, he was warned by his steward that Beira was a hell-hole, 'the sewer of Africa'. But it was surely never as bad as this. Today children and scraggy chickens scavenge in the gutters, pecking at foetid rubbish and dogshit and scratching at old tins, which may explain why even the eggs taste of rusty nails. The children will doubtless fend for themselves, but to be born a chicken in Mozambique would make one seriously question God's sense of humour. It's a brave man who risks hepatitis in the local restaurants, which are said to be leaping with salmonella or worse, and most Europeans seem to eat at home in shady air-conditioned luxury, cocooned behind high garden walls and fences in a curious black African variety of apartheid. After being warned about restaurant filth and flies I lived for a week on tinned South African frankfurters, tinned peaches, tinned peanuts, swallowing handfuls of malaria tablets, brushing my teeth in bottled mineral water and cursing myself for not insisting on a cholera jab before leaving London. Beira today is a great place for a diet: I lost half a stone in a week. The smartest place in town, the Yacht Club, is often without beer for days at a time. Even the chickens have to be imported from Zimbabwe, and the slimy, murky eggs refuse to boil even after five minutes, six minutes, seven. Edwina Currie would close the country down.

The monumental, stylish Grande Hotel (described when it was built in 1955 as 'a symphony in cement') is now a festering, blackened slum with trees growing out of the walls and squatters' laundry festooning the balconies. In the entrance lobby there is still a polite notice in English advising long-departed guests that 'the Reception Desk closes at 7.30 p.m.', but the squatters have ripped up the parquet tiles for kindling and a silent pool of sewage lies stagnant beside the ballroom where once the uniformed, be-medalled president of Portugal charmed fine ladies simpering in lace under the chandeliers.

Beira's elegant European villas are faded now and rotting with decay, the paint peeling, the windows cracked and smashed, the gardens scorched with squatters' fires. The tidy, picturesque Lusitanian squares are untended, the fountains dry. The louche, bustling nightlife of the old days exists no more and there is nothing much to do after dark. The Moulin Rouge nightclub, where once the yearning howl of the *fado* singers drifted each night across the Chiveve Creek, and where perfumed Portuguese prostitutes paraded for punters, is now a ruin, its forlorn red windmill sign in tatters. The six-storey 'Five Star' Don Carlos hotel at Macuti preserves its antique Portuguese furniture and paintings in a room that hums with the musty stillness of an old museum, but the hotel is often without electricity or water. The spacious Emporium department store (which boasted 'all the latest Paris fashions' in the 1950s) is now a warren of tatty shops. Outside it the heroic statue of the Portuguese colonist Caldas Xavier (1853–1896) has been replaced by a sad little representation of Mozambique's currency, the *metical* – plural: *meticais* – which is worth a thirty-fifth of 1p on the blatant black market. You can get 3500 meticais for £1, which is the average wage for a six-day week for African servants – a weekly wage that will buy them no more than a bag of apples or twenty eggs or sixty cigarettes. There were slaves here once (the Arabs used to ship them out by the hundred) and there are slaves here still.

A bicycle in Beira today costs five years' wages – £250 – and the rare proud tattered boy on a bike must feel like a millionaire. A good secretary earns £11 a week and even a judge makes only £20 a week. The local sixteen-page tabloid newspaper costs 1½p. It's main bingo prize is £2, and for a real Littlewoods-size windfall you need to buy a ticket in Mozambique's national lottery, which offers a first prize of £285. It costs only 10p entrance fee to buy your way into the 'exclusive' yacht club, the Clube Nautico. Unemployment is a way of life, and there's no dole. God knows how most of them live. The poor spread pathetic handfuls of shrimps on the pavement to dry. The fishermen's nets are empty but for a few gritty catfish. Children collect driftwood and sell tiny heaps of coal at the roadside, and their commonest plaything is a primitive toy: a stick wired to two empty tins which rattle around on their sides like wheels. How long can a child remain innocent in a place like this? On the beach at dusk a perky little black girl of about twelve flirts with me (*'Como está? Americano?'*) and I despise myself for knowing that I can't possibly give her any money, not here, not now, even though just £1 would make her skip with joy. She probably already has AIDS, which is said to have infected twenty-five per cent of the population and will kill millions in the next ten years.

Yet no one in Beira wears rags. There are plenty of cripples, men with one arm or one leg, heroes perhaps of the war of liberation or victims maybe of the Russian doctors, who are said to prescribe amputation like aspirins: it's a foolish Mozambican who goes to a Russian doctor complaining of impotence. But there are no beggars and little crime. Nor, amazingly, is there any racial bitterness. White faces are rare but they inspire only smiles and giggles. Tiny roadside children squatting over minuscule coal fires on the broken pavements, cooking unmentionable liquids in corroded cans, grin and call out as you pass, their dark eyes big and beautiful. Even the few decent surviving air-conditioned European houses are left unlocked all day (owned now not by Britons but by aid workers from Italy, Germany, Sweden, Finland, and by bewildered Russians wondering what on earth they're doing here when so much is going on back home). You can walk the streets alone after dark with a year's wages in your pocket and feel unthreatened, and you no longer hear screams coming from the pretty little white castellated prison where the fascist Portuguese used to practise their multiracial policy by torturing anyone at all, regardless of race, creed or colour. True, it is still dangerous to take photographs: the secret police are as jumpy as the Portuguese were. 'But you can't bribe the Mozambicans,' one white businessman told me. 'It's not like the rest of Africa.' When I left and tried to bring out with me a prohibited ebony souvenir (worth only £4) it was confiscated at the airport and the upright black Mozambican security guard treated my hint of a possible backhander with contempt.

*

Even so, it's a deeply depressing experience to return to Beira thirty years on. At the golf club old English cartoons from *The Compleat Golfer* and the mounted heads of antelope still hang on the walls, and two decrepit snooker tables survive in the billiard room, with old silver cups behind glass and honours boards listing championship winners since the 1920s. But no one plays snooker or tennis or golf any more: the clipped fairways and manicured greens are now a wilderness of waist-high grass and stagnant pools and marsh. On the other side of town the Beira Club is derelict, the roof caved in, the rafters a home for crows, the floors rotten. The fat leather armchairs are gone, perhaps to furnish distant thatched mud huts on the banks of the Buzi River. The billiard tables have disappeared along with the snooker cues and the framed Spy cartoons and the yellowing bound copies of *Punch* and *The Illustrated London News* from the 1930s. Beneath the Beira Club, on street level, where once there was a barber's shop where I went each month for a short-back-and-sides, a black hair-dresser still waits for customers in the sticky afternoon. But both his barber's chairs seem always empty.

Outside the old Savoy Hotel, now a faceless apartment block, where once in the 1920s a baffled hippo was found wandering in the street, there is still an old red English post-box, upright but gutless. At the Sunday service in the peeling little British church, where a stained-glass window still gleams in memory of my aunt's mother-in-law, there are 103 hand-clapping, chanting Africans – many more worshippers than ever there were in colonial days. The service is now in Portuguese and the old English prayer books of my youth are damp, rotting unused on the bookshelves: they crumble to dust when I open them, and scurry with spiders. The black children are amazed to see me sitting at the back of the church, the only white face there: they swivel in the pews and gape. Beside the font a photograph of their bishop, Dinis Sengulame, depicts a young black cleric with a luxuriant Jimmy Edwards moustache.

On the streets there are no pith helmets today, no creased Englishmen sweating in baggy white suits. The site of the Beira

Amateur Sports Club, where fat jolly Paul Westgate played Santa for us on the cricket pitch every Christmas and smelled of whisky, is now a stinking market. Paul Westgate has ended up buried in the quiet old Santa Isabella cemetery, where the water table was so close to the surface in the 1930s that the undertakers had to jump on to the coffins to stop them floating while the gravediggers hastily covered them with sand. Opposite the cemetery, where Paul Westgate now lies beside colonial stalwarts like Joe Simm and dear old Auntie 'Dunkeley' Leckie from Edinburgh, there is another cemetery, this one for abandoned buses, where dozens of vehicles with nothing much wrong with them are left to rot for lack of a few spare parts. No one seems to have thought of cannibalising a few of the buses to repair the others: lateral thinking has yet to discover Mozambique and cannibalism is no longer acceptable even here. There's still a half-built tower-block in the middle of Beira that has stood an uncompleted skeleton ever since the Portuguese were driven out fifteen years ago, and the Mozambicans seem incapable of even defending their towns against the guerrillas. They rely instead on the Russians, whose helicopters clatter overhead, and the Zimbabweans, whose armoured cars rumble through the suburbs to protect the city from the Renamo guerrillas in the bush beyond.

The bookshops sell nothing British at all, just absurdly cheap subsidised Russian books: the collected hardback works of Lenin for 18p, a garish paperback Soviet thriller for 13p. The São Jorge cinema, with its vast and vulgar tiled mural depicting England's St George and the dragon, where as a teenager I used to swelter in the back row and gaze with hot longing at Doris Day and Tuesday Weld in the 1950s, is now the Third of February cinema and screening a Slav film. The roundabout outside, once called Piccadilly Circus, has been renamed the Place of the Third of February (Mozambique's Army Day) in honour of the Frelimo heroes who died in the war of liberation against the Portuguese.

The airy verandah house where I spent my childhood and adolescence, where I wrote my first short stories in the steamy afternoons and produced a childish daily newspaper thanks to the BBC Overseas Service, and bent over the crackly radio to listen to distant commentaries of England/Australia Test matches, is today a squalid dump, shabby and neglected. The back yard is littered with rubbish, this trim arena where hundreds of African stevedores and clerks used to gather every Boxing Day to solicit small Christmas tips from my father, betraying their ancestors by giving him the roaring triple royal Zulu salute – *Bayé-té, Bayé-té, Bayé-té* – as he stood smiling and nodding like George VI on the little kitchen balcony. The oasis of lawns and shrubs created so lovingly by my mother has reverted to desert. The brick terrace laid so carefully by my father, the fountain he built, the aviary, the miniature Chinese garden, are now under concrete. 'The cement cost us a million meticais,' boasts the Indian owner's nephew.

A million meticais: £285. Just £285 to bury my past. No wonder the dogs here all howl at 9.30 every night.

Once there were Chinese faces everywhere in Beira: the portrait photographers clicking away in their little shops in the warren of streets called Banyan Alley, where the air was musky with the odours of cloth and spices and in back rooms old men played Mah-Jong. There were oriental market stalls, restaurants doubtless selling dog-meat, delicate hand-wringing merchants smoothing thin fingers over silks and caressing ivory ornaments and camphorwood chests. Creased yellow faces bent over games of draughts on the pavements. But now they have all departed, along with the frogs that used to croak incessantly from the grassy marshes beside the Chiveve Creek. Oddly enough there seem to be no mosquitoes either, despite the warnings of malaria. In my childhood we were lulled to sleep every night by the whine of bloodthirsty insects dive-bombing our mosquito nets in vain. Perhaps the frogs ate all the mosquitoes. Perhaps the frogs were all eaten themselves. But where have the Chinese gone?

Still, all is not quite lost, not yet. There's no television in Beira, for a start, which must be a sign of promise. And the hungry children will doubtless remember their childhoods as nostal-gically as I do. The huge red sun still explodes into the clean paw-paw coloured sky each day at dawn out of Madagascar, a yard above the horizon in ten minutes, to become a blazing arc-lamp by 7 a.m. The sea is gradually eroding the shore and exposing the sandy roots of the casuarina trees, but the huge empty Indian Ocean beaches at Macuti are still deep shim-mering white in the haze of noon, the lacy palms lazily stirring in the breeze beside the glittering sea. Frolicking black boys float on the waves in black inner tyre tubes just as we did so long ago. At sunset over the Pungwe River the golden clouds still glow with orange, then pink, then purple. The fishermen's silhouettes are no less poignant in the dusk. The black night still glitters with stars.

There are those who say that conditions are beginning to improve. 'If you think it's awful now, my God, you should have seen it three years ago,' said one Western businessman. The Marxist slogans are beginning to fade on the sun-baked walls and the EC is pouring in billions of dollars to reclaim Mozam-bique for the civilised world. 'Rehabilitation' is the buzz-word, and so much is being spent to modernise Beira's port, still vital for the tobacco and mineral exports of landlocked Zim-babwe and Zambia, that Zimbabwe's Minister of Transport and National Resources, Denis Norman, told me he believes that Beira could become one of the most modern harbours in Africa, a boom town again.

In the port of Beira copper exports are up by fifty per cent in a year. Just yards away from the rackety bus cemetery the Finns have installed a superb new satellite dish and inter-national telephone system, so that it takes just ten seconds to dial London or Stow-on-the-Wold and bounce your voice across the stratosphere, while pot-bellied children sift through the garbage ten yards away in the gutter. Even the Pope was here in 1989, preaching from a specially built wooden pavilion on the edge of the old golf course, waving his jewelled fingers at the mangy dogs. The pavilion, of course, is already a ruin.

The great fear now is that the West may divert huge amounts

of African aid to Eastern Europe instead, and that even if
Mozambique is helped stumbling to its feet again the effort
could be wasted if the 'rehabilitation' is handed over to the
Mozambicans to run themselves. 'These people can't think
of the future,' I was told by one dusky local businessman,
half-African himself, half-Portuguese. 'The Mozambicans just
don't care about tomorrow. It's not that I wish the Portuguese
were still here. The Portuguese weren't much better. I'm a
kaffir myself, and it takes one to know one, and the Portuguese
were the kaffirs of Europe. But I do wish the British were back.
Beira was a good place under the British. The British were the
best colonialists of all.'

CHAPTER 10

THE WHITE TRIBES OF SOFALA

IN THE MONTH before I returned to Beira the Renamo guerrillas had blown up the oil pipeline to Zimbabwe so often that 300,000 gallons of petrol and diesel had been lost. The British High Commission in Harare advised me to let the British Embassy in the Mozambican capital Maputo know exactly where I was staying in Beira 'in case anything happens', and warned me 'don't leave the beaten track': a week earlier eleven people had been killed when the guerrillas attacked a bus at Dondo, a village about ten miles from Beira once renowned for its grilled prawns and *piri-piri* chicken. Friends also warned me to be careful about taking photographs in Mozambique, where it is still easy to be mistaken for a spy: one of my father's successors as general manager of the Manica Trading Company in Beira had only just been freed from hellish Mozambican prisons after serving seven years of a twenty-year sentence after some oil tanks were blown up in Beira. Nothing had been able to save him from jail, not even the fact that when he was arrested he was the British Honorary Consul.

I had another reason for feeling nervous about my return to Beira: I feared that one of my novels, *The Spider and the Fly*, might turn out to be prophetic. Its hero is arrested and incarcerated in a particularly unpleasant African jail. In Beira.

Prisons played a major part in old Portuguese Mozambique, where the fascist dictator Salazar's regime was not at all squeamish about locking people up, not to mention torturing

150

them. In the 1940s and 1950s Beira swarmed with swarthy police-state officials festooned with epaulettes, gold braid, gold teeth, dark glasses and even murkier reputations, and when I was six I had to attend the police station to have my tiny fingerprints pressed into inky pads and registered by men with hairy fingers and devastating garlic grins. As late as the 1960s the Portuguese pressed Africans into forced labour – a new slavery – and a European could order his African cook or houseboy to report to the calaboose to be beaten for dumb insolence. But before that, from 1891 (when the old Arab harbour of Beira became the headquarters of the Mozambique Company) until 1947 (when The Company handed Beira over to the Portuguese), physical terror was better hidden, maybe because this sweaty corner of Portugal's primitive African empire was astonishingly British.

The old houses were built on stilts (to foil the voracious white ants) and the only drinkable water came from galvanised iron rain-tanks and had to be boiled and filtered before drinking. When my father arrived in 1928 there was only one car in the entire place (an Austin with the registration number B-1) and his Manica Trading Company building was like a Wild West bar with its verandah and hitching rail and in his early days as a shipping agent he handled exotic sailing ships like the Finnish barques bringing timber from Scandinavia. But there were 1000 Britons working here then, mainly on the railways, and there was great excitement when the Prince of Wales passed through in 1929 to catch the B.I. liner *Modassa*. Roads were given names like Paw Paw Alley and Suicide Corner, actors came out from Britain to put on theatrical shows, and the Beira Club was Mozambique's answer to Pall Mall: membership was restricted to senior managers, ships' captains and visiting VIPs; it is not difficult to imagine grim-faced colonial wives mortified because their husbands were not members. During the First World War the British ladies of 110-degrees-in-the-shade Beira knitted thick woolly socks for the troops in the trenches and they stood at attention for the National Anthem, and as late as the 1940s the British in tropical

Beira still lived like Edwardians. At dances, despite the sizzling heat, the men wore starched shirts and stiff collars and the ladies carried programmes (complete with pencils and gold tassels) so that they could be booked for cavorting later in the evening – for The Lancers, maybe, or quadrilles, the Military Two-Step, the Valetta. Well into the 1950s each Beira manager's wife, who had better be a consort of consummate rectitude or else, would have regular At Home afternoons (the first Wednesday of every month, perhaps) when anyone was welcome to call and partake of tea and tomato sandwiches with the crusts cut off, and fairy cakes, and Maids of Honour. Anyone *acceptable*, that is. It must have required immense courage for the wife of a junior manager to make her first call in the heady circles of senior managerial Beira society. When she left after her ordeal she had to remember to leave three visiting cards – one of her own and two of her husband's. If she returned a call only to find no one at home (or to find that the African servant had been instructed to lie that no one was at home) the three cards had to be left with their corners slightly folded over.

There was also a gloriously louche Edwardian underside to Beira life then. The midnight cabarets mournful with the guitar nostalgia of the Portuguese *fado*. The Moulin Rouge nightclub with its red sails glowing after sunset. The Penguin nightclub with its unlikely refugee Hungarian Gypsy Orchestra. The brothel (opposite the Sports Club) which my Aunt Dolly Leckie tells me was staffed by 'sweet little French tarts with poodles', young whores who took a great delight in trotting in and out of Dolly's red-faced husband Jack Leckie's office to contribute to the charity he ran: 'his staff thought he was paying them off!'

Even those who were lowly clerks and typists remember those days with affection: one of them tells me that they had great fun at surprise parties, when they would turn up singly or in couples at some unsuspecting bachelor's rooms until there was a vast crowd and the victim began to panic that he didn't have enough drink and snacks for them all, which was the signal for the 'guests' to produce their own bottles and food. It is easy today to denigrate such simple turn-of-the-century pleasures, but many years later my father wrote in his unpublished autobiography of 'the warm spirit of friendship' of those days and a friend of my parents, Mary Mitchel, tells me: 'there was magic, enchantment'. Certainly the adventurous spirit of those working-class and lower-middle-class Britons was admirable. They gambled with their lives by emigrating to seek their fun and fortune thousands of miles from home, beyond the equator, in a steamy town a foot below sea level where dozens died of malaria and blackwater fever and the cemetery seeped with stinking swamp water and ladies were banned from funerals because the burials had to be interrupted while the coffins were opened at the graveside and the corpses sprinkled with quicklime.

When in the 1930s my uncle Roger Lord was stricken with appenditicis the local Portuguese doctors confessed that this was too much for them to handle. They packed his stomach in ice and despatched him by train to Rhodesia, to Salisbury Hospital, 350 miles and twenty-four hours away. There the surgeon Godfrey Huggins (who later became Prime Minister and Lord Malvern) was appalled by the ice treatment and ordered hot water bottles instead. Against all the odds my uncle survived (he is now eighty-five) and there is indeed something indomitable about those early Mozambican Britons who have survived to tell me about their young days on the edge of that eastern ocean so long ago: survivors in their eighties like my Aunt Dolly and her adopted brother Jack Harrison and their tiny Scottish friend May Davidson, who was born in 1900 and still lives in a little flat in Harare but is as sprightly and enthusiastic as a sparrow as she shows me her unpublished diary of the old days in Beira and old photographs and newspapers from the 1940s. May Davidson lived there for more than forty years, doggedly staying on even after black independence, but was eventually forced to leave in 1978, abandoning almost everything, even her furniture, without any compensation from the Marxist Mozambican government. Her lifelong home has now been taken over by strangers, but she seems quite casual about it, shrugging her shoulders, not bitter at all. I would have been incensed.

Even in 1990 the tiny Cessna, bulging with a full load of pilot and six cramped passengers, takes nearly two hours to chug across half a continent from Harare to the coast. It is Shrove Tuesday but no one is serving pancakes. Despite the growl of the engine the five other passengers, all white, pretend to sleep all the way, among them a shifty, moustachioed Dutchman and a couple of sinister South Africans, one fat and arrogant with huge clumsy feet and eyes as pale as a lion's. It is a glorious morning as we flutter over the edge of the Zimbabwean escarpment, where the plateau is lapped by fluffy low clouds frothing against the mountains like foam on the seashore. Over the lowlands of Mozambique, across the province of Manica and Sofala, is dotted grassland and jungle where the Renamo terrorists are hiding and being hunted by the Frelimo government troops and the Zimbabwean army: maybe somewhere down there, in a hut or a hideout, the kidnapped men lie terrified. Below us for half an hour a thin, grey, sluggish stream slowly widens as it meanders towards the sea and eventually I realise with a shock that this is the Pungwe of ancient memory, my boyhood river, the one Cecil Rhodes had to navigate to make his first visit to Rhodesia in 1891, where *The Times* correspondent was eaten by a lion in 1890 and sunbathing crocodiles still lie grinning in the mud. And then suddenly, there, in the distance, beyond the droning engine of the little Cessna, there on the hazy horizon, is Beira, camped embarrassingly tiny on a spit of land stretched out into the mouth of the river against the Indian Ocean. And right there under the wings, down there beneath the snoring Afrikaner, down there are the docks and harbour with miniature ships on a shiny toy sea and Dinky cars and Hornby trucks and Meccano cranes, the docks where my father spent most of his adult life and was probably happiest but where my beautiful young mother nearly lost hers in a terrible fire one night aboard one of the Clan Line ships, a furnace that left her with dreadful burns and mortgaged the rest of her life. There, on the northern bank of an unimportant little tropical river, in a ramshackle little African town: my childhood.

The sudden ferocious heat as the door of the Cessna is opened is a blast of glorious memory.

I am a confusion of emotions.

I simply cannot believe that I have returned at last after thirty years.

My childhood lies in fragments all about me and yet I do not even recognise the airport terminal, which is miles out in the bush but astonishingly large and plush, with echoing marbled halls. The airport handles no more than one or two commercial flights a day but it would not disgrace a large Western city. It is almost completely deserted.

Vic Ferreira, the operations manager with my father's old firm, the Manica Trading Company, meets me and drives me into town in the Manica van. We bounce and crunch over huge potholes, along an avenue of palm trees and rotting marshes, just missing African pedestrians carrying squawking chickens and damp bundles of clothes and rusty household implements, and the foetid stench of Mozambican life and the steaming tropical vegetation assault my nostrils with all the delicate aroma of a garbage truck. We drive past the seedy holiday bungalows of Estoril, where Rhodesians flocked by the thousand in bygone days in search of sun and sand and sea and exotic Portuguese pleasures, past the rundown Don Carlos Hotel and the red-and-white-striped Macuti lighthouse with the rusty wreck of an old coaster still parked in the sand at the foot of the lighthouse to prevent any further erosion of the beach.

Beira.

This is *Beira*.

Vic drives me to the spacious company guest flat, right next door to my aunt's old house beside the beach, with its cool nostalgic red-polished floors and Lara the smiling African maid, and we have an absurdly English fish-and-chip lunch beside the sea at the Clube Nautico, the 'exclusive' yacht club. The place is packed with dozens of stolidly munching Russian and East German 'advisers' sniffing the hot ocean breeze. After lunch he drives me to my father's old office near the port, the Casa Infante de Sagres, an aged colonial building with venerable verandahs and whitewashed arches and vast mosaics of cool blue-and-white tiles in the entrance hall depicting heroic scenes from Portuguese colonial history. The building is now partly occupied by a health clinic where black patients lie on the verandah beside the dusty road.

The sauna heat is unbelievable: an assault.

I had forgotten.

I am dumb with nostalgia.

Later I walk back through the town to the Manica Trading Company flat, through the tired, well remembered streets and the baking afternoon, along what was once the trim Avenida da Republica, past the skinny dogs panting in the sandy shade beneath the acacia trees, where the temperature is only a hundred degrees, thank God. Unfathomable stinks waft out of the gutters, the sewers, the dark hidden corners of decaying old colonial buildings, and forgotten names suddenly surprise the surface of the memory like Loch Ness monsters rising to blink in the light: forgotten names like Casa Bulha, or Ramchand, or Pohoomul Brothers, the Indian shops down 'Banyan Alley' where stylish British colonial wives used to buy all their cottons and satins and silks to feed to their hungry Singer sewing machines fifty years ago in the endless empty breathless afternoons.

Outside the old Portuguese Government House, the *Residência*, where strutting young Lusitanian bureaucrats in white sweat-stained uniforms once shouldered golden epaulettes the size of ingots, a glowering black teenage soldier waves me across the road with his rifle in case I might glimpse Mozambican state secrets through the peeling, sunburned gateway. The potholes are vast, the pavements erupting with the gnarled roots of ancient acacia trees. Everywhere there is a stench of rotting, and the old colonial villas even in the centre of town are ramshackle and black with damp and decay, their windows broken, their paint discoloured, their verandahs and souls deserted, their grubby gardens fertilised only by scrawny chickens and snot-nosed children scuffing the sand.

Suddenly I am depressed and appalled as I realise what this place has become. Even St George's Memorial Church, which was raised to the memory of the British dead of the First World War, is now shabby and neglected, the garden a spiky desert – the church where my aunt and uncle were married in 1935, where I learned my alphabet in the vestry in Margery May's little nursery class in 1947, where at sixteen I listened to the new nineteen-year-old Missions to Seamen padre Bob Morgan's sermons before he and I attempted to seduce Carolyn Thomas and Kathy Luternauer on the beach by the Oceana Tea Rooms.

In just four hours of my first day here the magic and excitement have evaporated. This is not even the Third World. They said I should never come back, and perhaps they were right. My colourful dreams of thirty years ago have become grey snaps in black and white.

In Beira I came across a 1970 guidebook to the town which makes the place seem unrecognisable today. Inevitably street names were changed after independence: the Avenida do Presidente Craveiro Lopes is now the Avenida Martires de Revolução; Araca da India is now the Placa de Indepêndencia; and with splendid irony the Avenida Oliveira Salazar (in honour of Portugal's fascist dictator) is still named after a dictatorial regime but this time a Marxist one (Frelimo). Nor is it surprising that the Portuguese imperial monuments have gone, like the elaborate fascist concrete monstrosity opposite the Casa Infante de Sagres which commemorated the visit here of Presidente Marechal Carmona and carried a portrait of him and a coat of arms. But the guidebook's photographs are really depressing. The cover shows an immaculate central square by the bank, with lawn, trees, shrubs in flower, lots of cars, decent roads, a proper pedestrian crossing, and delicate pink-and-white buildings in good order. There is a strikingly glamorous picture of the Grande Hotel, and the São Jorge cinema (1200 seats) and the Nacional (1000 seats) are described as 'two of the most luxurious cinemas south of the Equator'. Today they are all slums – the central square, the Grande, the São Jorge, the Nacional – and of all the houses built here and cosseted by the British and the Portuguese no more than thirty decent homes are left. The rest are slums too. There are no taxis. You can't hire a bicycle, let alone a car. You can't even buy a bunch of flowers.

It would be quite wrong not to admit that some things in Mozambique today are actually better than ever they were under the British or Portuguese. Thirty years ago a white driver could kill a black pedestrian without too much embarrassment: the dead African would probably have been found guilty. Nowadays, I was warned when I borrowed a car, 'you don't stop if you kill a black child on the road: drive straight to the police station or you'll be lynched on the spot.' And Africans are free at last to share all the facilities that whites have long enjoyed – or at least those facilities that remain – from the bars and beaches to lavatories and swimming pools. In fact the only racists here nowadays are the dogs: those owned by whites still snarl at blacks, but those owned by blacks are now brave and independent enough to take great pleasure in savaging whites, and never mind the rabies. And the huge crows that strut along the beaches manage to be both black *and* white.

The Europeans here today certainly seem at first to be a very different breed from those I knew so long ago. The women especially seem horribly bored, with nowhere to go and nothing to do. Two of them tell me that they and their husbands never go out anywhere, not even to the cinemas or restaurants, which are now apparently so filthy that you need gloves to read the menus. There are no parties, no nightlife, and they seem to know nothing at all about the place, not even the banking hours or the fact that the Clube Nautico has a swimming pool or that the Pic-Nic restaurant is now closed. I have to show them where the Emporium is, even though its name still stands large and bold above the street. Their air-conditioned homes have become cocoons. Yet are they really so odd, or is it simply the debilitating effect of this energy-sapping place? My Edwardian mother too, I remember now, lived in a sheltered domestic world here, rarely venturing out. Maybe that has always been the secret of keeping sane in Beira.

'It's a huge challenge battling against all the African bureaucracy and stupidity,' one local European businessman complained. Another told me that the delays here are so immense that it once took him more than three years to cash a cheque for £80,000, and the bank paid only the day-of-issue exchange rate and no interest. The tallest building in Beira is a twelve-storey tower block of slum flats, and after fifteen years of independence there is still in the middle of town an unfinished Portuguese skyscraper that the Mozambicans have somehow not yet managed to get around to completing. Yet the British used to make similar complaints about Portuguese inefficiency. Certainly not everything has changed by any means. In the daily paper, the *Diário de Moçambique*, the lead story is a decidedly unMarxist one about President Chissano doing nothing more than meeting Princess Irene of Greece in Maputo. Outside the towns the ordinary black Mozambicans are starving, ravaged by war, disease and terrible famine, but whites here still enjoy Zimbabwean steak and chips, chicken and peas, prawns or tuna, macaroni, wine, coffee. They can buy almost anything at all in the hard-currency duty-free shop so long as they have American dollars or South African rand and can afford the prices: Tuborg lager at 40p a can, White Horse whisky at £5.70 a bottle, baked beans at 45p a tin, frankfurters at 91p a tin, a jar of jam at 80p, a tin of asparagus tips at £1.42. Even without hard currencies you can use Mozambican meticais to buy petrol at 70p a gallon, a John Lennon LP record for £1, a Coca-Cola even in the Clube Nautico for 34p, an ebony ashtray for 71p or an intricately carved ebony paperknife for £1.28. If you take a chance and change your money on the black market everything becomes about two-

and-a-half times cheaper: i.e. petrol at 28p a gallon and a bottle of scotch for £2.28.

And as the days pass and I begin to excavate my roots I keep unearthing traces of long buried memories of the white British tribe that once ruled this foreign field. No one here wears white suits or khaki sun helmets any longer, but in the club-house the honours boards still list championship winners since the 1920s, among them my uncle Lewis McDowall (who won the Governor's Trophy in 1930) and ninety-year-old May Davidson, the ladies' tennis champion in the 1940s. Nearby, on the wall of the golf club bar, there hangs an old coat-of-arms from a visiting British warship, HMS *Lynx*.

In St George's Memorial Church there is still a plaque that reads: 'This Church was Built to the Greater Glory of God and in Grateful Remembrance of those British Subjects formerly resident in this Territory who made the great sacrifice for their King and Country in the Great War 1914–19. Splendid they passed the Great Surrender made.' The atmosphere is gloomy and stifling, but the same gold cross stands on the altar just as it did thirty years ago, and the same Alpha-Omega altar cloth with a red cross on a white background, and the organ and font are still there and the same four wooden overhead lights and three big ceiling fans and the same green hymn books published in 1957. Perhaps even the plastic flowers are unchanged, just dusted down once a decade. Listed on the hymn board are hymns 78, 64, 45, and 83, and I look them up in the hymn book and don't know any of them, but the notice board still announces in English '7th Sunday next before Easter.' Beside the altar a bright stained-glass window glows deep in the sunlight with reds, golds, blue, green and brown and commemorates my aunt's mother-in-law, Margaret Leckie, with the motto 'Behold I stand at the door and knock' and a picture of Christ wearing a crown, cloak and sandals and knocking on a door. Beneath His feet is written: 'In Loving Memory of our Mother Margaret Leckie 1874–1958 Erected by her sons John & George.'

In the derelict beachside Miramar restaurant a sign by the

loo still says 'Ladies'. The Bank of Mozambique, once Barlclays Bank, still has a Barclays sign on the counter, and two of the black Mozambican clerks speak immaculate English. There is even a Lloyd's of London agency where an eager young African employee begs me to help him to become the BBC correspondent in Beira. His middle name, absurdly, is Jones, and he speaks excellent English. In fact young black men here speak better English now than young whites. One local eighteen-year-old European, José Oliveira, who speaks in a pronounced Rhodesian accent, has just passed his A-levels at his very British school in Zimbabwe but replies to almost every remark with 'is it?' as though English were for him an utterly foreign language.

'I lived here thirty years ago,' I tell him.

'Is it?'

'My aunt lived right next door to your house for many years.'

'Is it?'

I feel as though I am speaking to Mr Spock from *Star Trek*.

The present general manager of Manica in Beira, Jan Hendrikse, also seems at first sight an unlikely successor to my very English, pink-cheeked father. Jan is very different: tall, skinny, very brown, withdrawn, a forty-seven-year-old Dutchman with a rasping Afrikaans accent. He spent seventeen years at sea and earned a Master's ticket at thirty before joining Manica and serving in South Africa, Zambia and here. Yet he has much in common with my father, and like him is obsessed by ships and the sea, and works ridiculously long hours, and loves Beira, especially waking early and watching the tropical dawn come up and the early silence and the sea. He still works in my father's old office on the first floor of the Casa Infanta de Sangres, which he is having repainted: the workmen have had to scrape a half-inch of old green paint off the walls, scouring my father's past. My Dad is still remembered here by a few with affection and respect, by a couple of Manica office workers, by the Harbour Master, by a Goanese woman on the wharf, but the life that he knew has evaporated, and his white tribe now is no more than a pale flicker of ghosts. Its successors, the grim grey Russians 'advisers', have enjoyed an even shorter glory. They still pilot the ships in and out of the harbour, and their helicopters still patrol the guerrilla-threatened hinterland, and out at the airport big Soviet planes marked CCCP glide along the runway as grey and sleek and sinister as sharks. But their day is already over, too, after just fifteen years: Mozambique has turned its back on Marxism far more quickly than it did on the British and the Portuguese, and these Russians must be completely bewildered to be here so long after their own liberation from the shackles of Lenin, so long after *glasnost* and *perestroika*. They still sit sipping sticky drinks, cherryade, appropriately red, in the Clube Nautico, but their empire too has come to its end, and soon they will follow the British and Portuguese and go home.

The Europeans will still be essential, even paramount, in Mozambique for a long time to come, but they will be a new breed of white tribe. Hardware alone will no longer be enough in this hard Fourth World. They will also need hard heads, hard hats and hard currency – and probably very hard hearts.

CHAPTER 11

THE HOUSE OF THE LORDS

I KNOW NOW, thirty years on, that my childhood home was just a very ordinary three-bedroom colonial house, built on brick stilts, with a small garden, a red corrugated iron roof, veran-dahs defended by wooden blinds and mosquito netting, and floors of cool polished red tiles or parquet blocks. But for me for three decades, as I moved restlessly around England from one place to another, in and out of thirteen homes in thirty years, it symbolised stability, security, sanctuary, and family warmth. In Beira I had suffered that apparently dreadful handicap for a writer, a happy childhood, and I dreamed of that house and its colourful gardens, its pond and fountain, its aviary of budgerigars and lovebirds, the verandah room where we would all sit together at night and play Canasta and listen to the BBC World Service and the news from London and Mantovani. Remembering that room I can still smell my mother's 4711 perfume and the evening aroma of my father's cheroots and can still hear the gramophone and Richard Tauber singing *We'll Gather Lilacs* while the frogs and crickets croaked and chat-tered outside, demented by lust. I dreamed of the parties my parents had given for visiting ships' captains, and of the baby grand piano on which my sister fingered proper music and I toyed with *Chopsticks*. I dreamed of the verandah where I played card-cricket and typed my first childish stories and magazines in the stillness of tropical afternoons – of the magi-cal basement room where dozens of yards of Hornby Dublo electric train track and stations were set out on a huge single-

163

O-shaped table complete with homemade villages, farms, roads, trees, fields, fences, rivers and papier mâché mountains and tunnels. I dreamed too of the cartoon murals that my sister had painted on the green tiles above the bath: the fat-cheeked cartoon fish and the grinning octopus. But sometimes I remembered also the dark corridor where there had seemed to be some sort of Presence at night; and the bedroom where as a very small child I had had weird out-of-the-body experiences when I seemed to float in the corner of the ceiling and look down at myself; and I dreamed too in despair that everything had been changed and that my home had been despoiled in the years since I had left. After the Mozambican war of independence I heard rumours that no fewer than eight families of squatters were now living in our old house and that it was now a derelict hovel, and as late as 1985 I was imagining in my novel *Time Out of Mind* how melancholy it might be now:

> It's a rambling ruin with broken windows, cool once with veran-
> dahs and breezes but now gloomy with overgrown vines and
> creepers in the drawing room and tropical weeds sprouting mon-
> strous from the walls. I can see the sky. The roof has fallen in.
> The quiet is like Sunday afternoon.
>
> There was music here once, and laughter, and clinking glasses.
> A baby grand piano stands rotting in one corner, with mushrooms
> growing on it ... There are animal droppings on the faded old
> carpet. Two huge insects are mating on the mouldy sofa ... The
> world lasted for ever, then.

Friends warned me not to return and I suspected that they might be right: in *Time Out of Mind* I had also written 'I know now that looking back is always a mistake.' But eventually I could no longer resist. It was a way of caressing my memories of my parents, both of them dead for more than twenty years, their tropical ashes scattered into the icy breezes of Bourne-mouth. And there were other spectres in my head that could only be laid to rest by disillusionment. I needed not only to neutralise the obsession. I needed to find out. I needed to *know*.

I approached the house on foot in a sweaty afternoon daze just five hours after landing at Beira airport, turning off the main Avenida Eduardo Mondlane (once the Avenida da Republica but now named after Mozambique's first black President) down the Rua do Comandante Gaivão, past the farmacia on the corner and the old radio station next door, now filthy and derelict.

I still could not believe I was here again at last.

In a daze I approached the red-roofed garage where my father had for years parked his smart green 1950s Pontiac. Two Africans were sitting on the garden wall by the garage gate, idly swinging their legs, and I was baffled to see how low the wall is, no more than three feet high: as a child I had thought it was so big, a bastion against the world. The pergola my father built forty years ago is naked now, bare of any creepers, the tired metal glinting in the cruel sun. The side lawn is sparse and sandy and the scarlet and pink poinsettias that he loved have gone, long dead too. By the front gate I noticed with a shock that the house is numbered 205. How sad: how ordinary; I had always assumed it must be number 1; what else could it possibly be? And why 205? It's a very short street with just three houses on each side: where are the other 199 addresses? The front lawn, once immaculate turf where we used to play croquet and bowls, is dreadfully overgrown. The three huge croton bushes beside the house are stunted and straggly, their striped leaves of yellow and red quite shrivelled away. The red roof is faded and peeling.

It was too hot to weep.

I seemed to have no tears.

The place was completely silent, apparently deserted. The side garden, once a private secluded oasis of leafy bowers, pond and fountain, with a generous twittering aviary of flashing yellows and blues and a miniature Chinese garden of tiny pagodas and bridges, has been cemented over. Where my father toiled like Churchill for weeks every Sunday afternoon to lay a brickwork terrace of careful herringbone design there is now only a brutal slab of concrete decorated with a few strings of chicken wire. And the world looks in from beyond the low boundary wall.

Had everyone stared in then at my childhood? Into the green oasis where we had seemed so immune from the world? Surely not: surely we had been hidden then by vast hedges long neglected. And was it really this small and insignificant, my whole world then? How could my father have spent thirty-three years here – and loved it? How could my mother have borne it? How did my sister and brother and I ever dare to dream, here in this primitive sandy equatorial marsh, of London and Cambridge and Fleet Street and St Martin's School of Art? And how could I possibly have imagined such magic here that for thirty years I dreamed so often of returning?

Just beyond the front garden wall, on the corner of the empty Rua do Comandante Gaivão, a traffic robot blinks endlessly from green to red to amber, on and off and on and off for hours. It is utterly pointless: hardly anyone here has a car, and there isn't any traffic, and it's far too hot to *walk* unless you're some lunatic Englishman who has just arrived and doesn't know any better.

As I went away down those mean streets, past the piles of festering rubbish in the gutters, I felt afraid. My heart was pounding. Mad dogs and Englishmen: keep out of the midday sun.

I could only think that sweaty afternoon how glad I was that my parents are dead and never knew the fate of all their love and labours, and I prayed that at least at 205 Rua do Comandante Gaivão there are no bewildered ghosts.

For three more days, while I tried to make arrangements to meet the owner of the house and to see inside, I was drawn back to it irresistibly, returning again and again past the old Radio Beira studio next door, once the loudest station on the dial but now abandoned and squalid with squatters and stench, its battered doors hanging crippled on their hinges, its lines of tattered laundry gasping in the still air.

Beyond the radio station, beyond our old garage, clattering sounds came from the kitchen where Tope Sabiti (our little Nyasa cook and a local Muslim priest) once reigned over the Aga and the cheese soufflés and argued with me about God. For years we wrote to each other after I had come to Britain and he had gone back home to Nyasaland (Malawi) where my father sent him a regular pension and where his letters were obviously written for him at great expense by some pavement scribe. When my father died in 1969 Tope wrote me a letter of such deep sorrow that I still have it, and later I sent him a Christmas present each year. Yes, of course there was racism during the heyday of the British Empire, some of it exceedingly unpleasant, and our wash-house 'boy' was an elderly man unaccountably known to us only as Sixpence, but there was also respect between the races, and affection, and I remember not only Tope and Sixpence and Francisco and Makalassi but also my special African friend, the 'houseboy' Customo Bili, who left me feeling bereft after he was sacked for stealing whisky. My last two letters to Tope, in the late 1970s, went unanswered, and other enquiries came to nothing; I had to assume that he too had died, this good black man who served my family with devotion for more than twenty years and who was kind to his two wives and their many children and to a pampered white boy who was so much more privileged and lucky than his own sons.

Surreptitiously I photographed the house and garden from every angle, keeping the small camera hidden as much as possible, whipping it quickly out of a plastic British Airways bag from Heathrow – CLICK! – and stuffing it back again, afraid of being arrested, trying to keep out of sight of the head-quarters of the secret police right across the road. A couple of passers-by frowned suspiciously as I tucked the camera hurriedly into the bag, one of them stopping twice and turning to stare. Black children approached, and one boy giggled and pointed at the British Airways bag as the film suddenly ended and the automatic camera whirred loudly back to the beginning of the cassette. He followed me along the road, calling after me, past the front gate, the front garden, past the secret police headquarters, and then two streets away he pointed proudly at a rotting hovel that had once been an elegant Portuguese villa. *'Minha casa,'* he boasted. ('My home').

Yes.

For him too for decades that childhood home will doubtless be remembered as a beautiful refuge.

On the third day the tiny, birdlike Indian widow who now owns number 205 Rua do Comandante Gaivão, Senhora Bibi Umarjee, a mother of twelve, agreed to show me around it.

It was a devastating experience.

Just inside the front door, on the left, where my parents greeted so many guests so long ago and the little Indian lady now smiled at me and nodded, neither of us able to communicate much except by gestures, there are now set into the verandah wall some Portuguese tiles with four bouncy doggerel verses on them, the first of them reading jauntily:

> *Limpe os pés, descuidadão!*
> *Bem sei que não reparou! ...*
> *Mas o seu 'peço perdão ...*
> *Não limpa o que já sujou!*

(Don't come in with half the garden
On your shoes, you careless pup!
Use the mat! Just saying 'pardon'
Isn't going to clear it up.)

Also screwed on to the front door today is a plate with some unintelligible Muslim or Hindu slogan, and hanging over the Portuguese verses inside are portable Muslim or Hindu mottoes. Was it always this dark and gloomy? I remember this front verandah as being large, spacious and airy, but it's not: it's cramped and dull, a verandah (God forgive me) for a little

Indian widow, not one for a man like my father, an OBE, an Officer of the Order of the British Empire.

The same green wooden slatted blinds are rolled up over the mosquito netting, but now there are narrow beds cluttering the outside room where we played Canasta and listened to *South Pacific* and Charlie Kunz and the England–Australia Test matches and the news on the BBC Overseas Service with the chimes of Big Ben from London and the rousing nightly theme tune of Radio Newsreel – 'this is London: here is the news' – which crackled thousands of miles around the globe and brought us close to the heart of the Empire and made us feel part of the British family.

My sister's old bedroom is tiny and the lavatory in her bathroom is now just a hole in the floor. The 'ghost' corridor where we shivered and scurried for safety after dusk as as dark as night even in the bright tropical morning. As I stood in my parents' old bedroom, where once we would jump into bed with them in the mornings and feel so secure, tears pricked my eyes. On the wall above where their bed used to be, where my mother would lie in the itchy equatorial afternoons and beg for the terrible swollen burns on her arms and armpit to be tickled for relief, there are now garish glittering pictures of mosques that shift and shimmer like kaleidoscopes. No trace of my parents remains except in my father's dressing room, which is fitted still with his white wood cupboards, on one of which there still gleams in the darkness as dull as memory one glinting metal letter, L: L, for Lord. In the narrow corridor beside the dressing room the telephone too is in exactly the same place and has the same number as thirty years ago, Beira 3223, even though the correct number is now 324871.

Downstairs in the basement the Hornby electric-train room is now a five-bed dormitory, no doubt because of those twelve Indian children. The bathroom is now divided into two, and my sister's murals of fish and octopus have disappeared. The adjoining loo is once again mysteriously no more than a hole in the floor. In the kitchen the Aga has gone and a fat Indian woman sits cooking in the middle of the room with a primus

169

stove and a frying pan. Tope Sabiti would have a fit to see his kitchen like this. The back yard, where my father accepted so graciously on Boxing Days the royal Zulu salute is now all concrete. But how strangely selective is memory: in the middle of the yard is a deep old well that I had completely forgotten. Why had I forgotten the well yet remembered things that were never there, like elegance, sunlight and space? Could it be that my memories are completely inaccurate? Have I simply imagined that the front lawn was once beautiful smooth green turf? That we were all as happy here as I have been convinced until now that we were? Is it possible that my childhood was not so idyllic after all, that this house was always glum and dreary even then, that this filthy town was always godforsaken and inefficient?

No, surely not: it's undoubtedly a rubbish dump now; in the back yard there are careless rusty cans, litter, squalor, and it was never squalid when my parents were here. This was once a stylish colonial home where ships' captains and chief engineers and smart businessmen from the City of London were happy to come for sundowners and parties and dinner. Now it's just a Fourth World dump.

Senhora Umarjee smiles and smiles and smiles, like the Queen Mother.

On the following day I tracked down her forty-three-year-old son, Ibraimo Umarjee Adamo, in 'Banyan Alley', in the clothes and trinkets shop Moreira e Silva (where my mother bought cloth, thread and ribbons) that he has run since his father died in 1979. Next door is the Chinese photographer's studio (now an Indian photographic shop, but without any films for sale) where we had all our family portraits taken and the individual Polyfotos for passports and all those bureaucratic Portuguese residence permits and documents. Adamo is a delightful man, endlessly smiling and obliging, and told me that his mother has lived in our old house at 205 Rua do Comandante Gaivão for twenty-six years, since 1964, when his father bought it (for just £7,500) from one of my own father's successors as Manica

Trading Company general manager. His mother has five sons and seven daughters, three of them living now in Lisbon and two in Blackburn, Lancashire, of all places. So they too, like my sister and brother and me, have gone out from this same warm childhood home to scatter across the globe. This forty-three-year-old Mozambican Indian shopkeeper and I, and his brothers and sisters in Lisbon and Blackburn, were all raised and loved on that same small patch of earth and shared the same back yard and similar happiness and memories. There are two Indian women somewhere, among 10,000 homes in Blackburn, Lancashire, who understand my childhood.

On the day before I left Beira for good I made a final visit to 205 Rua do Comandante Gaivão and noticed that it is so many years since the front gate was opened that both its bolts are immovable and completely jammed with rust. Visitors now use only the tradesmen's entrance. Senhora Umarjee, undoubtedly one of the most tolerant women in the southern hemisphere, allowed me in again to copy the wording of the jokey blue-and-white Portuguese verses on the tiles on the wall of the front verandah just inside the front door.

When I write them down I suddenly realise how uncannily appropriate they are:

> *Com três letras apenas*
> *Se escreve a palavra mãe*
> *É das palavras pequenas*
> *A maior que o mundo tem.*

> (Mum's the word.
> Three letters do it.
> The smallest noun
> Has greatness to it.)

Mum's the word: whose Mum? Mine? Ibraimo Adamo's? And the third verse is so relevant that it might almost have

171

been grouted on to that wall decades ago specifically to teach me something now in 1990:

> *Pobresinha a nossa casa?*
> *Palácio dos sonhos meus,*
> *O teu amôr, e dos filhos,*
> *A graça e bênção de Deus.*

> ('This may seem like a hovel,' I nod,
> 'But to me – I'm a simple old sod –
> It's a palace of dreams,
> Of love, children and schemes
> And the Grace and the Blessing of God.')

I wrote them down.
    I stared at them.
    I understood at last.
    Senhora Bibi Umarjee has lived here in this beloved home of mine and hers for twenty-six years, for nine years longer than I did so long ago. While I have abandoned it and betrayed it and travelled the world, she has worn it comfortably for more than a quarter of a century. It is now much more her home than it was ever mine. She can do what she likes with it: how can I dare to complain? She is loved by her children and grandchildren as much as my mother was, as I am. My obsession has been absurd, and the spectres are laid to rest at last, and I will dream no more ridiculous dreams. Senhora Umarjee and I are soulmates, for this house has lodged in her heart as well.

CHAPTER 12

BESIDE THE INDIAN OCEAN

Dawn Over Madagascar

AT 4.30 a.m. a cool, damp silence loiters on the shores of the Mozambique Channel, a deep expectant hush as though the Earth were holding her breath. Nothing moves, not even a breeze. The silhouettes of palm trees stand motionless along the coast, dark sentinels watching the sea.

At 5.30 even the electricity suddenly cuts out and the air conditioning shudders into stillness, waiting. A yellow gleam lingers along the rim of the Eastern sky. Twelve black fishermen in six frail canoes paddle past along the shadowy coast towards the open sea, dwarfed by a distant dredger. Their patchwork sails, rough hessian maize bags stitched together, glow gold in the dawn. The sky turns the colour of mangoes, then pink with a mauve tinge on the horizon, then pale blue fading into the angry glaring white of a furnace.

And up it comes, suddenly out of the ocean, as fast and awesome as a rocket from a nuclear submarine – the sun, the 6.15 equatorial express, always on time, a blazing god surging from out of the waves. The feathery palm fronds tremble in the blast of its breath and the last wisps of cloud scatter nervously in its sight. From all over the town a chorusing choir of cocks is crowing hosanna. In Beira the sun's daily reappearance seems a miracle: one of the few things that actually work.

A lone man is exercising on the beach, bowing towards the East. The sun splashes the beach yellow, the clean clear light

173

of dawn glistening on the hard damp sand of the low tide and sparkling on the rivulets of retreating ocean and the driftwood, the empty can of insecticide, the plastic jetsam of civilisation.

The majesty of a dawn in Mozambique is impossible to exaggerate. The sun comes up from beyond Madagascar like a sudden red balloon on an upward thermal, like a molten bullet, a foot high in five minutes, a yard high in ten. One minute the horizon is just a dull, watery glow of pale yellow and blue, the next it is a white furnace ablaze with the glare of a blinding television arc lamp.

At 6.30 the electricity trembles back to life and I make tea with bottled mineral water (for safety) and powdered milk (there is of course no fresh milk). The resulting beverage has the most disgusting cloying smell and sickly taste. I try the shower in the stained, rusty bath, but the water merely trickles. Both taps in the basin are marked 'H' but neither produces anything more than a brief glurp of cold water.

Lara, the maid, arrives at 6.30 each day and I seem to have lost the knack of having servants. In fact it's decidedly irritating having someone in the flat all the time: whenever I walk into a room she always seems to be there, a dark ghost flitting permanently just out of sight. Perhaps the old colonial wives had a point when they complained that having servants was worse than doing everything yourself. No wonder British wives here often seemed neurotic and jittery.

Much to Lara's disapproval I still can't face the slimy fishy-smelling eggs of Mozambique with their disgusting metallic taste and I breakfast instead on a revolting mixture of tinned broad beans and Russian sausages on toast, and quinine tablets – or on bread, jam, tinned peaches and quinine tablets. Outside in the gutter there are children eating no breakfast at all.

By 7 a.m. the sweat is already dripping off me and my clean shirt is mottled with damp patches. My face is so wet that it's almost impossible to use my electric razor. I venture out to enjoy the cool of early morning but within half an hour I am sweating furiously again and the sun is blazing in a deep blue sky, already way up above the tops of the tallest palm trees, a ball of molten white fire too powerful even to glance at.

Teams of children are scouring the beach, collecting drift-wood, and just a few yards offshore fishermen and women are shrimping, trawling the edge of the sea in pairs, wading waist-deep, ten feet apart, with poles and nets gripped between them, to collect a tiny shrimpy sludge, no more than two handfuls each time. Later they scatter their catch to dry at the side of the road, a net of pathetic pink wisps strewn on the pavement, a slippery hazard for all the cripples and the limb-less who emerge at this time of day like maimed morning commuters to hobble by the beach.

I walk into town, through the Ponta Gea district of Beira.

Morning in Ponta Gea

There are no other whites on foot and Africans stare in sur-prise, good-natured but curious, and children gather and giggle. The vision of a white man walking here is obviously as rare as the sight of anyone at all walking in Los Angeles, where they sometimes arrest you on suspicion simply for being on foot. When I say *olá* or *bom dia* the children just stare or giggle and hide their faces.

I carry no more than £15 in meticais but the pockets of my shorts bulge with the worthless things, great fat wads of them: thirty 500-meticais notes (£5) in my back pocket, thirty in the right, thirty in the left. I rarely spend any of it except to buy the daily newspaper and the occasional beer: apart from trink-ets and souvenirs, anything else worth buying is only available for hard currency. It is ironic that despite South African apart-heid and South Africa's past encouragement of the Renamo guerrillas who have plunged Mozambique into bloodshed and famine, the South African rand is still more acceptable in the local shops than the British pound, even though Britain is pouring aid into Mozambique and helping to train its army. There's gratitude. And the duty-free shop is packed mainly with the goods of the very countries that have caused Mozambique to become as poor and miserable as it is today: South Africa and Portugal.

My wads of 500-meticais notes were all acquired in an apprehensive black market currency deal in a seedy little backstreet shop where a shifty Indian moneychanger lurked in the dark behind a makeshift cardboard screen and surreptitiously gave me 75,000 meticais for 100 Rand (double the usual rate) and no fewer than 2,000 meticais for just one miserable American dollar. I expected to feel at any moment the horny black hand of Mozambican officialdom suddenly hot on my neck and to face ten years in a Mozambican prison but I was told that 'everyone does it, even the police' and left the shop with a solid two-inch-thick wad of filthy 500-meticais notes in my back trouser pocket. Meticais don't merely rhyme with 'petty cash': that's all they are, too; yet those grubby bits of financial confetti, worth just 14p each, would bring joy in Beira to the faces of the beggar children who hang around outside the duty-free shop helping white shoppers to load their purchases into their cars.

You can of course spend the local currency at the racketty, ricketty wooden stalls of the chaotic African market. There, for meticais, you can buy green tomatoes, flyblown fruit, Zimbabwean cigarettes at 30p for twenty, sinister looking eggs for 57p a dozen. But the place stinks with hellish hot smells of drains and stenches both animal and fishy, acrid sweat, filth, refuse, disease. I try not to breathe. One day when the stench was especially foetid I wrote:

Recipe for the Beira atmosphere
Take one chamberpot of warm urine. Add sundry portions of faeces (dog, cat, chicken, goat, human). Add stinking fish, bad eggs, rotting fruit, and a pinch of marsh gas. Place in oven at Regulo 6 and bring to simmering point. Turn up central heating to 120°. Switch on oven fan to simulate occasional welcome but warm sea breezes. Remove all clothes. Place head in oven, over chamberpot, and breathe deeply.

Amazingly some Europeans do come to shop at this stinking market, even for food, even haggling over the prices. One white woman complains loudly that the apples are too expensive at 90p for a bag of ten. In another market, this time indoors and slightly cleaner, there is still a disgusting stench and unmentionable liquids oozing and squelching underfoot. Or is it perhaps even worse in countries like Bangladesh? Am I simply too British and fastidious and spoiled? Perhaps most of the world does live like this and would not be at all appalled by it. Outside the duty-free shop there is a dead rat on the pavement. By the sea wall the road is collapsing completely and on the other side there is a graveyard of a dozen rotting, rusty hulks propped up against the wall.

The port is a restricted area, defended by soldiers, but I am given the right introductions and manage to get in to talk to the Port Captain and the Harbour Master and to sniff those old nostalgic whiffs of animal hides and timber and to see where my mother nearly died in that terrible fire in 1953, where now the Italians are building a new berth.

Back in town I buy the daily paper, the *Diário de Moçam-*bique, for 1½p. It is printed in Beira in Portuguese, a sixteen-page tabloid with red spots and diamonds dotted about irrelevantly in the middle of news stories and you have to cut the top edges of the pages yourself, though it is actually better printed than the appalling Bulawayo *Chronicle*. On the front page there's a big picture of Nelson Mandela in Lusaka and the lead story reports a speech by President Chissano attacking the lawless Renamo guerrillas. There is also a headlined picture about starvation in Ethiopia, perhaps to persuade the Mozambicans that there is somewhere even more hungry and miserable than Mozambique itself.

In a souvenir shop I find a use at last for my meticais by spending some of them on presents for people in England: a beautifully carved wooden paperknife and a delicate ornament of three ebony palm trees with detachable branches and leaves. The gifts are ridiculously cheap: £4 for both. But will I be allowed to export them? Other travellers have been accused of 'stealing Mozambique's heritage' by trying to take souvenirs out of the country. 'Just bribe them in customs,' says one white woman airily, but it doesn't work: when finally I leave Beira both gifts are confiscated at the airport.

By 11 o'clock it is far too hot to be walking anywhere under this broiling sun. My shirt is soaked, a wet dishcloth, my face awash with sweat, which careers down my glasses like rain on a window pane. I head for the beach (and the only breeze in town) for a drink with young José on the terrace of what used to be the Oceana Tea Rooms: two beers and a Coke for just 60p. A ship is coming into harbour around the headland by the derelict Grande Hotel. Two African boys, face down in the sand, are stalking tiny crabs for lunch. An old black woman with shrunken breasts is beachcombing, half-heartedly collecting a bundle of spindly twigs that will burn for no more than thirty seconds. Is she really so old? In fact she's probably no more than thirty-five, but she looks like a great-grandmother: how do these people endure the pain and sorrow of their lives, the absence of hope? Six children with sacks are together collecting driftwood with greater organisation, maybe to sell: they have the energy of entrepreneurs. Soldiers in camouflage are cooking over an open fire on the edge of the road, their guns propped against their truck. They are probably not as ferocious as they look: in Mozambique it is quite possible that despite the weapons they have no ammunition at all.

The low tide has exposed the skeletons of old wrecks buried deliberately decades ago deep in the sand to prevent erosion of the beach: they sprout from the beach like rotting teeth, or like Robinson Crusoe's stockade. The terrace of the Oceana Tea Rooms is a place of nostalgia: it was here in my spotty teens in the 1950s that I would bring girls at night in the vain hope of seducing them with omelettes, Fantas, the latest hits on the juke box (six months later than the rest of the world, of course) and the sensuous sussuration of the sea on the shadowy shore. It was there, right there beside that rusty, rotting, barnacled wreck embedded deep in the beach, that I

178

first kissed my first love, Virginia le Grande, the dark exotic half-French girl from the Seychelles, just beyond the dawn.

'I used to come here a lot when I was your age,' I tell José.

'Is it,' he says.

It is idyllic now on the beach with the low tide sucking quietly at the sand, the blinding sun and blue water, the twinkling rivulets trickling down shallow little channels in the deep white sands, the shade of the palm trees, the black children splashing joyously in the sea beside the laughing girls and women (the new arrogant black middle class, the wives perhaps of army officers) who are calling imperiously for a carafe of wine from the waitress at the Oceana. It looks so tempting and I want to swim too. But only fifty yards away there is a terrible stench from the open sewer that runs raw into the sea. There are whites here who refuse now to swim in the sea because they are terrified of contracting AIDS from the water. 'What if they pee and I swallow some?' says one woman. The doctors say it's impossible but I know exactly how she feels. Even the sharks refuse to swim here any more: on this beach thirty years ago you could often spot their black fins hovering three or four hundred yards offshore and although no swimmer was ever attacked you never spent too long under water without surfacing to scan the horizon. Now there isn't a shark in sight for miles: the pollution has driven them all away; they have gone to wherever the mosquitoes and Chinese have gone.

Noon at Macuti

The best place to swim, as it always was, is on the remote Macuti beach a few miles out of town, a few miles nearer the clean salt water of the open ocean, by the old red-and-white striped lighthouse where two coasters have been wrecked deliberately on the beach to prevent erosion. The road to Macuti is the worst of them all, with massive potholes and deep drifting sand. But the beaches are lovely, wide and white and deserted, the stuff of travel brochures. Here at midday even the lizards dare not move in the midday sun. Macuti is a picture postcard of glittering sea and gleaming sand dunes, of Africans asleep under frilly casuarina trees in the sultry silence of the tropics at noon. But the beach is hot enough to make you dance and any European foolish enough to expose his naked body now without protection would be raw and raving after an hour. It is even too hot to swim until the sun begins to dip into the Pungwe River and the evening rollers start crashing in from the Mozambique Channel.

Macuti was always the favourite spot in the 1940s and 1950s for the 6000 landlocked Rhodesians who would flock each year to the coast for their holidays (and at Easter and for every Rhodes and Founders weekend) to stay in the holiday camp chalets, the camping site or the Estoril or Don Carlos hotels. The camp has been taken over by squatters and squalor and the Estoril is now a slum, though the '5-star' Don Carlos still has a faded Portuguese grandeur in its big dining room and musty lounge with its old paintings and murals, Portuguese ornaments and knick-knacks and a sign that reads: 'Please don't move the furniture.' Over the lavatory door it still says 'Homens – Gents.'

The lighthouse is also now such a slum that you tremble to imagine how unreliable its lifesaving beam might be out at sea during a storm on a wild black African night. Parked at its foot is the older of the two wrecks, that of the good ship *William Eggots*, which was sacrificed in 1918 and driven brutally ashore to save the lighthouse from the sea and was doomed to end its life as no more than a swimmers' open-air changing room, rotting and rusting, a dark red crumbling skeleton leaning at forty-five degrees into the pounding Indian Ocean towards the rising sun. When eventually the old ship became too frail to protect the beach and lighthouse any longer alone it was given a younger mate, a fellow sacrifice, the perfectly named little coaster *Macuti*, which was obviously destined by its name alone for this maritime graveyard where now it too is half buried nearby in the sand, broken-backed, rusty and desolate in the glitter of noon, spewing its guts out under the broiling sun, its old boilers askew, its pistons and wiring rotting with salt in the pounding surf. Two old vessels as broken and weary as Mozambique itself.

Beyond the deserted headland with its huge rollers breaking on wide white sands, a distant fisherman faces the ocean breeze alone and the empty shore beyond Macuti towards unknown territory and the dangerous coastal strongholds of the rebel Renamo terrorists. In the empty afternoon it is easy here to imagine being kidnapped.

The Cock in the Afternoon

By 1 p.m. the heat is shimmering on the beach. The sea itself seems a mirage, its wavy image dancing as demure as the lacy palm fronds. The humidity is exhausting and so ferocious that even indoors each room feels like a Turkish bath. Black children are playing outside happily bareheaded in the sun, yelling in the street and frolicking on the beach, naked, splashing in the sea, unburnt. How did any European ever manage to do any work at all in this heat before the arrival of air-conditioning? How did we do our homework, or revise for exams? Colonials used to complain of the Africans' idleness, but how else could anyone be in this heat but exhausted? No wonder so many colonial women turned to Bridge, gin and adultery. No wonder we revelled in the rainy season, when each afternoon brought blessed relief with a sudden relentless thunderstorm, the deluge sometimes coming down in sheets, ten inches in twenty-four hours, a tropical downpour rapping on the hot tin roofs.

We coped with the heat in the 1940s and 1950s by taking sticky two-hour siestas and although in 1990 I tried to revive myself with a lunch of ham sandwiches or tinned peaches it was impossible to resist the temptation to doze for a couple of hours each day after lunch in the cool bliss of a darkened air-conditioned room. Even the chickens sleep here twice a day and the cocks crow again in the afternoon.

When I was a teenager a favourite escape from the afternoon

heat was to scurry into the air-conditioned luxury of one of the three cinemas and gawp at the shape of American actresses like Sandra Dee but not one British or American film was being screened when I returned in 1990: the movies now are from Bolivia, Yugoslavia, Morocco, India. At the Olympia Cinema (where I saw my first film, *Bambi*, in the 1940s) the posters are hand-scrawled now and the interior is acrid with old sweat. The São Jorge has inside the same old pink and blue murals on the walls of its broad foyers but the stink in the auditorium is staggering, the musty unwashed stench of Africa. The red-white-and-black foyer carpets are the same as thirty years ago but they are threadbare and patchy and have been stitched together so often over the decades that parts of them, especially on the steps, are now more thread than carpet. Horsehair stuffing hangs out of the foyer chairs, and the glass display cabinets no longer advertise forthcoming attractions. Instead they show numerous posters of Camarade Presidente Samora Moises Machel – Mozambique's Lenin – who led his nation to independence in 1975 and became its first black President but died in 1986 in a mysterious airplane crash in South Africa, some say the victim of the Afrikaner government, some say the victim of a complicated Soviet plot. 'The poor mourn your death,' cry the posters in Portuguese, 'the struggle continues – *A Luta Continua*.' By odd coincidence this week's film is called *Luta des Trafficantes*, an East European movie (starring Janós Kovác) that looks as though it's about drug-peddling: there are garish stills of some tough-looking crooks. I think I would prefer Sandra Dee and Tuesday Weld and all those other Hollywood fantasies that tormented my tropical adolescence.

British boys undoubtedly grew up much quicker than we did intellectually but the equatorial heat matured us sooner physically: certainly I was sexually aware from about the age of eight, when I appalled my mother's half-caste seamstress Clara (who must have been in her twenties) by looking up her skirt while she slept and admiring her long smooth coffee-coloured legs. From the age of eleven or twelve those endless steamy, sweaty, airless afternoons were a sticky turmoil of inflamed longing and lust: the heat, the heat, the heat, especially during those long silent siestas when the sheet stuck to your skin and even the breeze was paralysed. There was a desperate shortage of girls (the Portuguese ones were guarded like virgin princesses) and there was little alternative but to lick your lips over the prim pin-ups in the yellow weekly bound editions of the *Daily Mirror* that arrived by airmail from London and to sublimate all that frustration by writing stories, typing homemade newspapers and magazines, playing model soldiers and card cricket, or experimenting with the little Adana printing press ordered from London and imported at vast expense – anything at all to forget the desperation of unattainable sex.

Not much seems to have changed. José too, at eighteen, has no girlfriends here. 'I have to wait till I go back to Zimbabwe,' he says.

'Is it,' I reply with grim pleasure.

One shameful afternoon when I was a spotty fifteen and travelling back to school in Rhodesia by train I wandered out of my first class compartment along the corridor through the second class carriages and spotted in one compartment a pretty mulatto girl of about the same age, a complete stranger, who was sitting with her family. She caught my eye as I passed her compartment and immediately left her family and followed me down the narrow corridor to another compartment. There we said nothing, not a word, not even our names, but the urgency was awesome behind the locked door as the steam engine panted and shuddered and the train swayed across the Central African plains. Later, when she had left me, I was filled with exultation and shame. When I walked back past her compartment she looked away and her little brown father stared at me with granite eyes as cold as hopelessness: he knew, I'm sure, but there was nothing he could do; I was the young Master, the young white *baas*; I had merely fulfilled yet again the ancient rapacity of my race.

*

Dusk Over the Pungwe

After siesta, as the heat eases and the sun dips towards the
Pungwe River, the sea still glitters but the breath of Hell has
cooled. The sea is tinged grey with a froth of scum, as warm
and murky as mulligatawny. Two fishermen paddle in to shore
in a tiny ten-foot canoe and spread their nets on the sand to
dry. They seem to have caught little, a cat-fish or two, but small
groups of Africans gather around each net, staring at nothing:
they have seen nothing in the nets before, I expect, and will
see nothing often again. As the afternoon fades a swim in the
warm pool at the Clube Nautico is a delight as a breeze begins
to whisper from the sea. A black athlete is running around
the pool and doing exercises: Mozambique for the Olympics,
maybe? Outside, on the road, a albino girl with African features
but very pink skin and ginger hair looks understandably lost
and morose. On the beach a skinny bearded Scandinavian,
probably one of the aid workers, lies on the sand and caresses
a black woman, licking her neck. Eventually he takes her
photograph. He must want her very much indeed: films here
are as valuable as cigarettes in Berlin in 1945.

By the Oceana the sky is a brilliant pink too and the pounding waves splash rainbow foam in the sunset across the
seafront road, soaking the crowds of wandering evening children and jogging soldiers (bloody joggers even here!). Rows
of Africans are fishing off the beach and groynes with simple
hooks, lines and no sinkers, just hand-held lines and a stick
pushed into the sand and perhaps a few small catfish hoarded
in a hole in the sand. When I was a boy, no Africans dared to
use these beaches but now they fish and swim here freely,
laughing and playing ball games, and teenage lovers canoodle
on the sand near the derelict, blackened, squalid Grande Hotel
just as Ginny le Grande and I did so long ago. The setting sun
beams low on the horizon over the Pungwe and Buzi Rivers,
giving the sky a glorious golden glow. A couple of hundred
yards past the Grande there's a secret lagoon beyond the headland, completely secluded, the water blue in the sunset, with

a wooden stockade exactly like Robinson Crusoe's. And some Man Friday has left footprints in the sand.

On the shore is a small shanty town, two canoes with canopies, two fishermen trawling waist-deep for shrimps, wading together with poles and nets through the quietly lapping sea, behind them the huge sun setting in a haze and a ship leaving harbour through the narrow channel behind a careful little Russian tug. In the distance the shabby old Portuguese four- or five-storey 'skyscrapers' give the illusion of city.

Then the sun sinks suddenly in a gentle haze over the thin land horizon on the far bank of the Buzi. It's a beautiful time of day, as lovely as dawn, with a stiff fresh breeze off the sea. There are Africans everywhere and rumbling buses packed with crowds of evening commuters even here in the tropical wilds. What do they all do? Where is there to go? Dusk falls quickly, like a black cloth suddenly dropped over a birdcage, and I am suddenly apprehensive in the gloom: shadowy Africans stare at me, the rare white man alone and on foot at dusk. The sun's rays shine pink and purple like torch beams over the mauve smudge and the grey wisp of cloud on the horizon.

In the gathering darkness I sit on a concrete groyne still warm from the day and let the filthy sea wash my feet. The waves pound against the groyne time and again, soaking my shorts, and will pound on for ever until it has ground the groyne to rubble. The shore is much more eroded than it was thirty years ago, the sea wall pitted, the trees standing stark and vulnerable, their naked roots exposed. One day the ocean will swallow Beira and even these sorry remnants will be gone along with the lost white tribe and the silver golf trophies and the polished tennis honours boards and waltzing at midnight at the old Savoy Hotel.

Fat white crabs scurry down the beach in the gloaming as the tide ebbs, scuttling for safety just as the fat white Portuguese did fifteen years ago when the tide turned against them in the twilight of their empire. I photograph the silhouettes of two black fishermen as the sun goes down behind them glowing orange beyond the pink clouds and the dark silhouetted palms of the Buzi River. Long after the sun has gone a fading golden glow remains. The breeze is magnificent after the stifling heat of the day. It is 6.45 p.m. and the sudden night has come down like velvet.

Black Velvet and Orange Flames

The nightly carousing in Beira was legendary in the 1920s and 1930s, in private homes, in the hotels, clubs, nightclubs and brothels. There were riotous private parties, Sundowner Dances at the sports club and balls at the Portuguese club, the Gremio, and you could board the liners in port and dance to the ships' bands. Indeed, Beira was renowned as a 'fast' place where the bars closed daily for only two minutes, from 23.59 to 0.01, to comply with the regulation that they had to be shut at least once a day. One wonders what the Africans thought of this, especially on New Year's Eve when every ship in harbour sounded its siren at midnight and every car hooted and the British wore silly shiny party hats and roared in their cars all over town, from the coloured fairy lights on the verandah of the Beira Amateur Sports Club to the elegant dining room of the Savoy Hotel, where Ruby Maclean and her band played the hits of the Twenties and Thirties (doubtless, in Africa, the *Black Bottom*) and there were crackers and streamers and they bellowed *Jingle Bells* to the clanking of syncopated spoons against Portuguese champagne bottles. Small, bewildered bands of Africans tried to join in the fun by wandering around town beating tins and empty petrol and paraffin drums but what did they really make of it all, the booze, the rich food, the luxury, the giggling white girls and their redfaced swains with loud voices and ridiculous penguin suits? Was it envy the Africans felt? Hatred? Contempt? I suspect they were simply wistful, only sad to be excluded from all the real fun and wishing that they too could afford to dine at the Savoy and drink champagne and dress their wives in silk and lace and roar around town tooting like Toad – poop-poop. At dawn on New Year's Day

186

the Europeans would drive out to the beach at Macuti to swim and to welcome the sun as it rose behind the lighthouse, a tradition that continued well into the Fifties. On my last New Year's Eve in Beira, in 1959, when I was sixteen and soon to leave, I found myself out at Macuti well before dawn and wandered away from the others to shuffle alone in the night through the crashing phosphorescent surf and to gaze at the sharp unflickering tropical stars, and I shouted at God in the deep black African night because I was convinced that I had just discovered the Secret of the Universe and the Meaning of Life and had heard the Music of the Spheres.

I hope my parents enjoyed a similar euphoria occasionally in Beira when they were young because one Saturday night in June 1953 – at the very time that the Queen Mother was touring Rhodesia – their happiness was kidnapped for ever by the harbour fire that nearly killed my mother and left her with horrendous burns from which she never fully recovered. She was only forty-two at the time, beautiful and lively, but because of the tragedy that night she was dead just thirteen years later, exhausted by suffering, and three years after that my stricken father followed her, felled by loneliness and grief. Yet my mother was one of the 'lucky' ones: no one ever managed to count all the victims but perhaps as many as 100 people, all but one of them Africans, were killed by the inferno that ruined her life.

My parents often dined aboard with ships' captains when their vessels were in port (at the time my sister and I were at boarding school in Rhodesia, my five-year-old brother at home with a babysitter). After dinner on board the *Clan Sutherland* on Saturday 27 June 1953, at about 9 p.m., they were about to leave the ship when all the five ships in the harbour suddenly went up in flames with a terrible explosion like a bomb blast: the Norwegian tanker *Fenheim* had been leaking petrol into the sea and the entire harbour was suddenly set ablaze by a spark from an acetylene welder torch repairing the bows of the *Clan Sutherland*. At least eighty black stevedores died on

187

the nearby Belgian steamer *Steenstraete*, suffocated by burning sisal, wool and goat hair as they slept down below in the hold under tarpaulins ready for the early morning shift. There were more explosions and for weeks afterwards black bodies were washed up on the beaches. On one ship those who tried to escape found the decks so hot that they hopped and skipped and danced and then collapsed, their feet already cooked meat before they died. At the moment of ignition my mother was stepping up from below on to the deck with one of the guests, Captain Starkey, the captain of the *Clan Macaulay*, which was also in port, when she was knocked down by an orange fireball and dreadfully burned. Captain Starkey too was burned but they managed to stagger ashore and were rushed to hospital. All the lights in the ship went out. My father and my uncle and aunt, John and Dorothy Leckie, who were luckily still down below, groped up to the deck to find the gangway ablaze. Two of the lifeboats suddenly burst into flames and my uncle grabbed a hose and played it on them as the fire raged.

A white man in white shorts staggered towards my aunt, saying: 'My God, I'm burned.'

'You'd better see the doctor,' she said.

'I *am* the doctor,' he said, lurching away. Later he died, the only European fatality.

There was a sickening stench of foul black smoke and burning rubber as the car-tyre fenders caught alight. 'Jump, Mrs Leck, jump!' yelled the Portuguese on the wharf at my aunt as the flames threatened to take hold, but the gangway fire was eventually extinguished sufficiently for her and the others to escape down the charred and smouldering steps.

My mother was in hospital for three months and was burned so badly on her arms and hands that for ten days the doctors expected her to die. She had been wearing a nylon dress that had melted in the heat and stuck to her flesh. The pain must have been excruciating. For days in that terrible heat she lay swathed in bandages like the Invisible Man, with only her eyes exposed, but by immense good fortune the Portuguese doctor treating her, the superb Dr Manuel Gonçalves Dias, had worked at the Mayo Clinic and telegraphed the clinic and Guy's Hospital for the latest treatment for burns. He and the wonderful Roman Catholic nuns applied gauze and ointment patches to my mother's scarlet wounds despite her cries of agony and gave her strength and nursed her back to life. She never forgot her debt to them. She told me later that soon after reaching the hospital she knew she was dying and wanted to die and was about to let go and give up the ghost when she had a vision of her children's faces and knew that she had to fight for our sakes: as soon as she screwed up her will to live the pain surged back through her.

My father continued to represent the Clan Line in Beira for seven more years but they never paid him or my mother a penny in compensation even though they must have been well insured. 'It was quite disgraceful,' says my aunt, 'but in those days you just didn't sue.' And my father had wonderful old-fashioned ideals about work and duty and loyalty: the Clan Line was part of his family of ships, and you don't sue your family.

Had it happened today my mother would probably be awarded a huge sum. She should at least have been given enough to keep her in comfort in her last years but she was given nothing and died in a rented house in Hampshire because my father could not afford to buy a decent house after they retired to England in 1960. His business contemporaries retired to big, comfortable houses but when he himself died in 1969 he left just £10,000 after thirty-three years of loyal, selfless service in Africa. He also left, of course, his OBE.

I hope somebody somewhere at some time felt guilty about this shameful injustice, but it doesn't seem likely. There is darkness everywhere, not just in an African night.

Back in 1990 at 7 p.m. the heat indoors soon wraps itself around you once again like a velvet blanket. The sweat begins to drip again even by the window as you listen to the pounding ocean and sniff the breeze and the nostalgic scents of a swelter-ing tropical night: ozone, bougainvillea, dogshit.

In the flat there is a dartboard in a little cupboard: Lara the maid, touchingly, has left the doors open, no doubt to make me feel at home. The darts themselves are displayed uninvitingly in the living room on a vulgar bar-counter decorated with heart, club, spade and diamond. It could almost be the public bar of a British pub except for the kudu head mounted on the wall and the lack of a television set. Down south in the capital, Maputo, television programmes are broadcast three nights a week but here, oh bliss, there is nothing – no *Dallas*, no *Neighbours*, no *EastEnders*. Disgruntled telly addicts have to settle for videos flown in from South Africa: the only nocturnal flickering here comes from the fluctuating voltage of the light bulbs and the gleaming phosphorescent foam of the sea; instead of the constant babble of television that afflicts every street of every civilised country every night of every year, the sultry nights here are heavy and silent. It's so quiet you can hear *other* people think, and until the demented crickets begin to click and clatter like castanets you can hear the palm fronds fluttering feathery in the tiny breeze.

Out at sea a crescent of navigation buoys winks green lamps to mark the narrow dredged channel into port. Along it two ships, one slowly leaving harbour, one slowly arriving, approach each other as nervously as blind men in a corridor. They twinkle bright with lights of red and white. I feel a strangely deep contentment: if my father's ghost is anywhere here it is no longer brooding over old injustices but is surely instead with the spirit of those twinkling vessels sailing the waters he somehow loved for so long.

Children's silhouettes flit along the groynes and voices float in the darkness, African families promenading in the evening air just as the Portuguese families used to promenade so long ago, seeing and being seen, the poorest families prouder than any, flaunting their meagre finery. How can Africa ever hope to shake off her European influence when ordinary black people, even the poor, even in a Marxist country, still insist on aping the imperialists?

By 7.30 it's already deepest night but I walk alone where

the waves plash frothy white on the sand and crabs scurry in the dark along the deserted seafront to the Oceana, unafraid now, unmolested, unthreatened, certainly safer than I'd be on the Underground in parts of London or the subway in New York. There is not another white in sight but the Oceana Tea Rooms are packed with laughing Africans (the rich in the disco upstairs, the poor on the barstools and verandah downstairs) and they are drinking (but not tea) and loud disco music booms across the beach. Has anything really changed at the Oceana since thirty years ago, except the colour of its customers? The disco lights flash red-blue-green-orange-red as energetically as ever the jukebox did with the warblings of Elvis Presley and Cliff Richard.

Back in the flat I struggle to write up my diary but it's so hot and my hand sweats so much that biro after biro keeps failing on the damp, slippery paper. At 9.15 all the dogs suddenly start barking, then whining, then howling – an eerie chorus that happens at the same time every night. I am baffled. Why should they do it? There's no lunatic full moon, only a slim silver crescent in a sky brilliant with sparkling stars, diamonds on black velvet.

At 9.30 the dogs all start howling and yapping again. Are they crazed by the heat? Maddened by witchcraft? At 9.55 it happens again, and now canine replies and echoes are coming even from the most distant parts of town so that I think I understand at last the origin of the term 'barking mad'.

At 10.30 the electricity supply comes out in sympathy and goes on strike for twenty minutes, by which time even the dogs are in the dark and quiet at last.

The low tide snores gently against the beach. Far out on the horizon the tiny red and white lights of a distant ship gleam in the night. Above are millions of stars, a million more than you ever see in Britain, and the half-moon glitters brilliantly, spotlighting the figure of an African standing in the garden by the back gate.

For two hours now he has been standing silent there in the dark, unmoving beside the gate, the silver moonspray of the

Indian Ocean glimmering on the beach behind his shadow. He has just been standing, looking at nothing, going nowhere. Is he a burglar? A suitor? Or the Manica night watchman, protecting us all from non-existent intruders and thieves?

What patience. Perhaps in the end that's what Africa really needs, just patience and resignation.

Or perhaps it has always had too much of it.

CHAPTER 13

DIARY EXTRACTS

I DON'T KNOW why I'm so surprised and depressed by the squalor. It's worse than it was but Beira was always smelly and inefficient and never exactly hygienic. In my own novel *The Spider and the Fly*, published in 1974, one character remarks of Mozambique: 'The original white man's graveyard. Try not to breathe too deep or too often. Stinking.' So why am I surprised? Why have I forgotten?

*　　*　　*

People sit around all day, on walls, in gutters, doing nothing. How do they live? They don't seem to care. It's an attitude, a philosophy of life, that makes the agonies of the British fifteen percent mortgage rate seem pretty trivial.

*　　*　　*

Even the blind man I saw today tapping with a white stick along the pavement outside the Bank of Mozambique (and it must be hellish to be blind in Mozambique) looked fed, clean and decently dressed. In Africa of course families are much more prepared to help their members than they are in the West, but how can families do anything at all if they have nothing? A mystery.

*　　*　　*

At 10.55 p.m. (8.55 in England) I telephone Stow-on-the-Wold. Stow-on-the-Wold: what a funny name it seems from here. The Cotswolds seem a galaxy and centuries away with their honey-coloured stone houses, neat lawns, narrow tidy lanes and narrow tidy people. The call is connected amazingly quickly as always: I can speak across the stratosphere like a god, yet ten yards from my door hungry children play in foetid puddles and the cost of my telephone call would feed one of them for a month. Should I give them money? Would it do any good? Of course it would: I could make a couple of urchins here euphoric for a year, like fat jolly Paul Westgate playing Santa at the old sports club at Christmas, just by giving them a few miserable pounds. But would that make them hate me, and hate the world, because I can give so carelessly without thinking about it? It would be wonderful to give a bundle of cash to some startled child but it would also be shameful: it would be playing games.

*   *   *

To the Post Office to buy postcards. The choice is very limited, just six awful, dull photos. I pick two types: one showing Africans pounding cotton and one of an African blowing a long twisty sausage-like 'musical' instrument. On the back of the second card it says in Portuguese *Feliz Ano Novo* [Happy New Year] and also (in English) 'Season's Greetings.' Since it's March the African customers gaze at me as though I'm completely mad.

*   *   *

I've been here only five days so far, but alone and in this heat I've already started talking to myself.

*   *   *

194

At 9 a.m. to St George's Memorial Church for the Sunday service. I introduce myself to the black padre, who flies up here regularly from Maputo. The service starts at 9.10 with just seven men, two women, three male teenagers, and twelve children but it fills up remarkably as time goes on. People keep wandering in, especially women with children, until when the last arrive (at 10 o'clock, an hour late) there are 103 in the congregation plus two priests and two acolytes. The congregation is as restless and noisy as a Greek Orthodox wedding. Mine is the only white face. The service is in Portuguese, the black priests in white with purple stoles. The priest drones on interminably for an hour and a half. A few punters go up for Communion and disgracefully I think of AIDS infection on the chalice and wonder who pays for the wine. Beside me a very helpful black man in pin-striped trousers points out the pages of the service to me. Women and girls are dressed in matching Sunday best. Everything is sung and chanted. The priest slurs his words ridiculously so that he is unintelligible. There is no organ or piano, yet I get a tingle down my spine when the third, fourth and fifth hymns sound like lively African tribal music and they start clapping and shaking hands and I find myself in the middle of a sort of religious Paul Simon *Graceland*.

Light streams through Dunkeley's bright stained-glass window beside the altar and tears prick at my eyes, not just for her or for my lost past but also for the simple faith of these people as they sing happily and cross themselves, and the children tinkle tiny, worthless coins into a collection bag, coins of such little value that I have never yet seen one so small even here: each coin must be worth only the tiniest fraction of a penny. What have these people to be happy about? Yet their smiling faces shine with grace. Surreptitiously I stuff a huge wad of my unwanted meticais into the bag, about £2-worth. When I wink at a couple of staring children they seem to disapprove of such levity.

Finally I escape at 10.45, unable to take any more, bowing hypocritically at the altar, as they all do when they come and go endlessly during the service, constantly moving chairs and benches, children scuttling from one pew to another. There is nothing pi or po-faced or tight-arsed Anglican about this lot. One group of boys is so crowded in one of the pews that a couple of them decide to move to another pew in the middle of the service, whereupon they are followed immediately by all the others, who cram also into the new pew so that it becomes just as crowded as the previous one, which is now completely empty. Is this stupidity? A jest? The priest takes no notice at all, just droning on and on. At the start of the service I am the only one in my pew but after about an hour I have to abandon it when the tenth adult tries to cram into it on the far end despite the fact that there are empty chairs elsewhere in the church. They are very stupid, yet also very touching, and they kneel on the bare floor. And there were never this many white people in this church thirty years ago.

*   *   *

To the seven-storey railway station that the Portuguese built in the 1970s and then forgot to blow up when they had to leave suddenly in 1975. Like the airport it is far too grandiose for a small town like this. Indeed, it is so absurdly impressive that there is a colour photograph of it alongside the Beira entry in the *Encyclopaedia Britannica*. It is huge and cavernous with high ceilings and proper raised platforms beside the single line to Zimbabwe. No trains run, of course, and there is not a train or a passenger in sight.

*   *   *

The tiny Cessna finally takes off from Beira only half an hour late on the return journey to Harare, the same six-seater that brought me here though the pilot is different. I'm very lucky to be on the flight even though there are only two other passengers, for two more have been told untruthfully that the flight is 'fully booked' and have had to drive up to Zimbabwe today through dangerous guerrilla-controlled bush. The reason for the lie, says the pilot, is that there is no petrol in Beira so the Cessnas now fly Harare/Beira/Harare rather than the other way round and there is not enough fuel for the return trip with a full load of passengers and their luggage.

As we lift off and head west along the narrowing Pungwe River, back towards Zimbabwe and civilisation, how tiny and insignificant Beira looks below and behind us on its distant little headland. And it is. I shall never return.

CHAPTER 14

BEYOND THE HORIZON

MOZAMBIQUE IS STILL racked by the bloody horrors of civil war, famine and an African brand of communism that went horribly wrong. The value of the country's exports has plunged from £163 million a year to just £50 million and the guerrillas' sabotaging of the oil pipeline and the railway has cost the country about £1 billion in lost revenue. But now that President Chissano and the Frelimo government have turned their backs at last on Marxism and are begging for capitalist investment, those who ought to know believe that as soon as the war can be ended Mozambican towns like Beira could boom again in a new golden age reminiscent of the 1920s and 1930s, the years when Mozambique was moulded by the British.

Western nations have started to pour money into rescuing Beira, and the landlocked Zimbabweans are doing all they can to rehabilitate the town, which is their nearest port and has always been for them such a vital access to the ocean. There are very few British still in Beira apart from some Lonrho cotton workers, but leading the Zimbabwean campaign to resurrect the town has been President Mugabe's white Minister of Transport, ex-senator Denis Norman, who has also for four years been chairman of the Beira Corridor group of concerned businessmen. When I met him in Harare and expressed my dismay at the ramshackle state of Beira today he chuckled:

'Compared with three years ago it's almost a haven. 'The railway line has been rehabilitated in eighteen months with relaid track at a cost of US$17 million, with a lot of the money coming from donors like Austria. We've spent US$850 million rebuilding the harbour and plan to spend US$450 million more. It can now take 100,000 containers a year and there's a new oil terminal and the channel has been dredged and there are new tugboats and marker buoys so that the port can now take boats of up to 60,000 tonnes. Last year there was an eleven per cent increase in trade through Beira, and by the end of 1992 its capacity will be five million tonnes a year. The World Bank will repair the roads and sewers and the Zimbabwean Cresta Group will refurbish the Don Carlos hotel.

'In ten years Beira could be a boom town. What we've got to do is to put back the basic structures. And there's no corruption in Mozambique.'

My father's successor as general manager of Manica, Jan Hendrikse, agrees that Beira is about to boom. It shipped 150,000 tonnes of Zambian copper in 1989, fifty per cent more than during the previous year, and will handle a great deal more as soon as the terrorised rail and road links are made safe again and improved. And Beira's Dutch port captain told me that the huge investments on the harbour will soon turn it into the best port on the entire East African coast.

The European Community is spending US$650 million rehabilitating the port, and the sixty dockside cranes that were built in Bath in 1929 and installed here soon after my father arrived are now being refitted by the Germans. 'The British should be really proud of those old cranes,' one worker told me. 'They still work.' The Italians are fast modernising the wharf, building smart new berths (including an oil berth) and installing facilities for containerisation and refrigeration. The Finns are providing the machine shop and repairs. Almost everyone believes that when the work on the port is finished (by 1993) the town could be transformed by new money.

Siemens have laid new electricity cables and the EC has promised a new road programme, which is described by one businessman as 'conscience money'. Even the Beira golf club is being 'rehabilitated' by a business consortium and the Italian owner of Sandro's Club in Harare, the local unofficial Press Club, is about to open a new venture in Beira with a clean kitchen and decent restaurant: it could make him a fortune.

True, everything here at present is still bought with Western aid and there are very few exports: thirty per cent is Zambian copper, seventy per cent is Zimbabwean tobacco, minerals and cotton, and Mozambique's own exports (of cotton, cashew nuts and prawns) are minute. And there is still widespread white cynicism about Mozambique's future, a fear that however much the West spends resurrecting places like Beira it will all be allowed to fall into ruin again as soon as the whites leave. It would be blinkered to dismiss these fears as being simply racist. 'It's impossible to teach these people anything,' I was told by one experienced white adviser who would not be here if he were a racist. 'I'm not being racist. They just don't care.'

Even more outspoken was the half-African half-Portuguese who calls himself what no one else these days would dare to call him, 'a kaffir', but who said bluntly: 'The kaffirs here will still need Europeans to run this place otherwise it could just be another disaster.'

Towering above the wharf is a huge French roll-on, roll-off vessel from Le Havre bristling with trucks, containers and machinery, the gleaming epitome of modern technology and efficiency. Beside it in the next berth is a Mozambican coaster, the *Chinde*, which is not only tiny but shabby – and stinks. 'Kaffirs,' says the half-kaffir, shaking his head. 'Just kaffirs, you see.'

Still, at least Frelimo has now abandoned its monopoly of one-party rule and promised free elections. Everyone agrees that criticism is now accepted here: you can openly criticise even Frelimo, though you can still be arrested for 'acting against the State' (by threatening to strike, say) just as you could when the fascist Portuguese were here. The Russians still pilot the tugs and helicopters but the East Germans are leaving and the Marxist slogans painted on the walls (*Down with Capitalism, Up with Socialism, Viva the National Education System*) are fading in the sun. It is ironic that at the very moment that Robert Mugabe is trying to persuade Zimbabweans to accept Marxism and one-party rule in Zimbabwe both are being abandoned and discredited as failures in neighbouring Mozambique and all over Africa. It would be even more ironic if Mugabe's suspicion of Western capitalism and Chissano's new embrace of it eventually produced a rich Mozambique and a poor Zimbabwe. Mozambique is a warning to Mugabe of what Zimbabwe might one day become.

EPILOGUE

WHEN I RETURNED to Britain in 1990 I wrote two brief articles about my African pilgrimage that brought an extraordinary response from Africans both black and white. A short version of Chapter 1 appeared in the *Sunday Express* colour magazine and a short version of Chapter 9 in *The Spectator* and I was inundated with letters from strangers as well as long-forgotten contemporaries and friends of friends. My requiem for the lost civilisations of Zimbabwe and Mozambique, my lament for the ghosts of King Solomon's mines, had struck some deep reverberating chord.

Ellen Afriki wrote from the Vumba: 'Hallo Pal, so how is it there in London?' Tambudzai Mutindimuri wrote from Mutare: 'Pass my tender and warm regards to the family, Yours in the name of Jesus . . .' Sir Garfield Todd was kind enough to write: 'Your article is very good – very sad – a terrible story.' I even received several letters from the wilds of Western Australia from the doctor who had delivered me, club feet and all, in the Lady Kennedy Nursing Home in Mutare forty-eight years ago, Dr James Montgomery, now eighty-five. Until then I had never heard of him.

I was also invited back to Mozambique to attend the celebrations to mark the centenary of the Manica Trading Company in 1992. And I was deluged by a flood of letters from the Zulu Head Girl of Eagle School, Glandeur Sibotshiwe, the first of which began 'Dear Mr Lord (PAL)' and the most recent of which began 'Graham Dear.' I would not be at all surprised to learn that she has taken up knitting. If anyone still doubts the power of the British legacy in Africa, Glandeur is now working for the Post Office in Harare and her address is in Pat Palmer Owen Drive, the Cotswold Hills. So much for the otherness of Stow-on-the-Wold, the Cotswolds, England.

But there were shadows too. No story really ends. In November 1990 Sir Roy (or Sir Raphael) Welensky had to have an operation and his shakes are now so bad that he cannot write. In December, much to the consternation of Zimbabwe's vital 4000 white farmers, who own thirty per cent of the country's arable land and provide fifty per cent of its hard currency, President Mugabe made the constitutional change necessary to allow him to nationalise white land and give it to black peasants. The civil war in Mozambique seemed no nearer to ending and the world's charities were begging for more money and warning that Mozambique was facing its most terrible famine yet. In November there were riots at the high school Sir Garfield Todd founded at Dadaya and several buildings were burned to the ground by senior students frustrated by high unemployment. And five months after I stood at Eagle on the site of the 1978 massacre of the missionaries, glad at least that such atrocities were over, a seventy-one-year-old farmer and his wife, Mr and Mrs David Wiggins, were murdered by unknown killers at their farm in the Burma Valley below the school. Mr Wiggins had been a vociferous supporter of Ian Smith.

Smith himself, that remarkable survivor, was in June awarded by Zimbabwe's Parliament $14,588 – not only every dollar of his unpaid MP's salary and allowances that he had claimed (after being suspended in 1987 for contempt of Parliament) but even interest and legal costs. The Speaker of the House who had refused Smith's claims for so long, Comrade Didymus Mutasa, had been quietly removed as Speaker.

And there was also of course that new Zimbabwean MP, who will doubtless go far, who announced that Zimbabwe should be immensely grateful that God had given it 'His Other Son, President Mugabe.'

My return to Africa was of course a classic Quest, a pilgrimage not only across the globe and into the past but also into myself. It was a spiritual voyage that I had already imagined in my novel *Time Out of Mind* (itself a poor substitute for the journey proper) in which the protagonist writes: 'I know now that looking back is always a mistake.'

Well, is it?

I don't think so. My quest was sometimes depressing and masochistic but it was also exhilarating – and necessary. It made me face reality and it laid the ghosts. Since returning to England from Africa the old dreams and nightmares have evaporated – though it's eerie to realise for the first time that the three most dramatic episodes in my story occurred within a few dates of each other, in June: the Queen Mother's visit to Eagle, the fire that tortured my mother, the massacre of the Eagle missionaries.

Any quest, especially one like mine into the fabulous lands of *King Solomon's Mines*, should end with the discovery of some treasure, perhaps some small new wisdom worthy of Solomon himself, at least a glint of gold amid the dross. I learned little, I fear, except perhaps to be a little more tolerant of Africa and Africans and their monumental struggles. Back in London I read again my father's unpublished autobiography *Essex Lad* and discovered that even in 1928, when he first arrived in Portuguese Mozambique, the local currency was just as worthless as it is today: he describes how he first went ashore in Lourenço Marques (now Maputo) and proffered a half-crown (2/6d) for his bus fare and had to hold out his hat to collect the change (in Portuguese escudos) because there were so many coins and notes.

I learned also not to idealise the past and to be a little less arrogant about my memories. How could I have forgotten that my mother's fire and the Queen Mother's visit had both happened within a few days of each other in 1953? I had had no idea. I was astonished to find my memory so distorted and to realise that my fantasies were utterly subjective. My childhood was idyllic, of course, because that is how I remember it, and that's what really matters, but I came to realise that it must also have been deeply lonely, the childhood of an outsider, and for that too I am grateful: that loneliness and feeling of alienation taught me to be self-sufficient and nur-

books. What any artist needs as a child is not unhappiness but alienation – a feeling of separateness, apartness, *apartheid* – what Graham Greene called 'a splinter of ice' in the heart.

What else could explain why my sister became a painter and illustrator, my brother an animated-film-maker, and I became a writer? Each of us was moulded not only by genes but also by a lonely but fabulous childhood in Mozambique and Zimbabwe, a gift more precious than all the gold of King Solomon's mines.

Ishe komberera Africa!
Amen.